LOVE APPLE ISLAND

~ For my best beloved ~

Sarnia Chérie, gem of the sea,
Home of my childhood,
my heart longs for Thee.
Thy voice calls me ever,
Forget Thee I'll never.
Island of beauty,
Sarnia Chérie

Deighton

Cover: Les Amarreurs, Guernsey
Photograph by Tony Ozanne

Yvonne (circled) at Vale School

Love Apple Island

... a life on the island of Guernsey

Yvonne Ozanne

Foreword by Roy Dotrice

ELSP

Published in 2007 by
ELSP
16A St John's Road
St Helier
Jersey

Origination by Seaflower Books, Jersey

Printed in Britain by
Cromwell Press, Trowbridge, Wiltshire

ISBN 978-1-903341-45-2

CONTENTS

FOREWORD
by Roy Dotrice

What a wonderful trip down Memory Lane this delightful book gave me. Yvonne has such extraordinarily evocative descriptive powers that I was transported back to the halcyon days of my youth on that idyllic island of Guernsey.

Yes, I also have sat with 'Fergie' in the Director's Box at Old Trafford, Manchester. David Beckham signed his Man United shirt for my grandson. But it still wasn't as exciting as that once a year confrontation with Jersey at The Track football stadium. I think it was the Guernsey Donkeys versus the Jersey Crapauds* wasn't it?

And (ah!) The Guernsey Greenhouse with its unique aroma of ripening tomatoes. When I was five years-old my neighbour's two daughters took me up to their Dad's greenhouse, stripped me naked and bathed me in the static water tank. Unfortunately I was far too young to appreciate the experience!

However, I do know that you will enjoy every word in this delightful book. I can assure you it will be my bedside companion for late night 'dipping' from now on.

Roy Dotrice
Hollywood
(ex-Le Foulon, St Peter Port, Guernsey)

* Crapaud is the French name for toad. Jersey has them, Guernsey does not.

INTRODUCTION

In 2000 I lived near Caen, in Normandy, France for six months, caring for my granddaughters whilst my daughter and son-in-law qualified as Advocates at Caen University. Whilst I was there I recognised the Guernsey we had been brought up in, our island life of the Forties and Fifties. The values, community spirit – even the beaches – seemed to be of a time I remembered that is now all but disappeared from our beloved Guernsey.

This book, including articles published in the *Guernsey Press*, is the result of wishing to share precious memories but also to think about Guernsey's future and the lives of our children and grandchildren.

I hope you enjoy my writing. If you do I will have succeeded and I am grateful to you all. *A la Prochaine!*

Yvonne Ozanne
Guernsey 2007

Acknowledgements

Thanks to many friends and family: to Tony Ozanne who always made sure I got things right. To Alison for her endless encouragement and Michael for his generous enthusiasm. Thanks to David Jones and Kate Green who always believed in me and to my mother, Mary Bréhaut for her lively contributions. Thanks to Emily, Penny and Gordon Dawes for helping Granny to achieve an ambition. Thanks are due to Di Digard, Features Editor and Richard Digard, Editor, for their kind permission to reprint articles first published in their newspaper, the *Guernsey Press*. To Roger Jones of Seaflower Books and Robert Bréhaut of Alternative Solutions who eased me through the technicalities of producing a book. Thanks to the many people and establishments who helped me with my research.

Last but not least, thanks to Roy Dotrice and all who have responded so positively to my writing. It is a pleasure and a privilege to live amongst 'the quiet nobility' of the Guernsey people and to belong to such a special place.

Yvonne Ozanne
Guernsey
October 2007

1 Coming Home

There is fear of foot and mouth disease. Our annual South, West and North Shows have been cancelled. This reminds me of Guernsey life, just after the Second World War. After living in Gloucestershire, we finally return. We initially stay at my grandparents' cottage in the Vale. I am five and have never seen them before. My first memory is of my grandfather. He is sitting on a window seat, wearing a soft fawn cap and a navy blue Guernsey.

He laughs, without making a sound. He is fair and his eyes are twinkling blue. He beckons to me and I go and sit next to him. Near him, at the end of the room, is a black range, fiery warm.

The mantelpiece is covered with a tasselled cloth. On it are two white, china dogs, facing each other, and a pendulum clock ticks slowly by. My little grandmother hands me a doll. It is wrapped in Cellophane. She has stored one for each of her granddaughters. A potbelly kettle hisses on the range. People are bustling about.

There is a long table, with benches either side. My grandmother lays the table, with bone-handled, two-pronged forks and heavy knives. Her dinner plates are white with blue patterns.

Just then, I notice a wooden rack, suspended from the ceiling. On the rack are strange forms, wrapped in muslin. These, my grandfather tells me quietly, are salted pork.

I do not know what he means. We children sit down to enormous, boiled eggs. When I cut the top off the yolk is bright orange. Duck eggs. Grandmother makes toast with a toasting fork by the range fire. We are home. Noticing I am shy, my grandfather asks me if I want to see the ducks. He carries me on his shoulders, past his greenhouses. On one side is a grassy patch where his ducks are quacking and chasing each other.

My grandfather selects one and tells me that it is mine. I can name her. I call her 'Poopy'. He laughs, soundlessly. From then on, grandad would take me each evening to feed Poopy Duck.

Even better, at the end of the garden were grandad's pigs. They were

11

wonderful, hairy animals. We were allowed to scratch their pink ears and backs, but be careful of their snuffling snouts. We would watch as grandad mixed the oaty brew, smelling deliciously of warm bran.

Adèle, Edwin and
Mary Bréhaut, 1915

Every pig was called 'Choog'. It was years before I realised that all the Choogs ended up on the rack in the kitchen. My grandmother made a meaty brawn and fine bean jar. So the Choogs had fed a growing family for many years. There was no central heating in the cottage, but I never remember feeling cold. The bedrooms were lit by gaslight, and very cosy. There was an outside lavatory, which was a bench with a hole in the middle. I always felt I might fall into it and disappear.

Yellow roses bloomed outside grandad's shed, where he packed his crop of tomatoes. This was a bicycle shed as well. Nobody had a car yet. We walked freely in the lanes, full of celandines in spring.

We flicked 'bread-and-cheese' at each other (really called Wall Pennywort) and threw a sticky weed onto woollen jumpers, shouting "Tick, tack, too. The devil's on you!" When we got stung by nettles, we'd rub the rash with Dockweed, which always grows near stingers. Sometimes, we would walk down the lanes to our great aunt and uncle's house – my grandmother's brother and sister. They kept chickens and we often had a boiled fowl for supper. Collecting the eggs was fun, because the hens pecked free, under the garden's apple trees.

On the south-facing stable wall grew pear trees and a cherry tree that never produced fruit. The front garden was full of cabbages. But, in the back, amongst the clay pots of red geraniums and nasturtiums, the pink dog-roses and pastel blue hydrangeas, great-uncle Alf grew soft fruit.

There were rows of purple blackcurrants, sweet, transparent redcurrants and hairy, green gooseberries. They had an ancient pump, surrounded by ferns and a deep well, where a spreading fig tree grew. When my great-aunt's pail clanged on the cobbled yard, the chickens clucked and the cockerel's cry met the still morning air, I thought these days would last forever.

Behind the house they had their own windmill. And, in the lean-to, their own noisy, oily, generator. Heavy black grapes hung overhead, whilst tomato plants thrived in their straight rows. We liked to smell the new seedlings, after they had just been watered. Enter the hot house, close the door carefully behind you, then breathe in!

The fresh young leaves gave off a humid scent good enough to eat. In winter, it was time to clean the soil. We'd follow the steam boiler down the lane to the vinery. The men would be laying the pipes, ready for the scalding steam. This heavy, hard work was shared among the growers. They would do shifts, all through the night. Each grower helped the other with men and goodwill. And the heady smell of steaming baked earth made up for it all.

But the heaviest vinery work of all was stoking the boiler pit with anthracite coal. We loved to watch the red flames leaping, the sparks flying. We'd sit on top of the boiler pit to warm our feet. My great-aunt always called, angrily, hating to speak English: "You'll get arthritis! You'll come to tink! You'll see!" We laughed at her. But she was right.

In 1958, Alderney did get foot and mouth disease. The trays of disinfectant at meadow gates and the signs FOOT AND MOUTH DISEASE – KEEP OUT, frightened us. We thought we would get it. We inspected each other's mouths and feet. What were the signs?

And so, we will have to wait until next year for our shows. The organisers promise that they'll be even better then. I'm sure they will be. They are an absolute joy. And they, at least, are still with us. For that, and for all they stand for, we offer great thanks.

13

2 Solidor

July 2003

Should we paint St James white, knock down the Eyebrow House, lose the Old Prison and our Market? Outsiders might wonder why we make such a fuss about these things. Well, it is because Guernsey people have stakes on this island that go down so far they are part of its very soil. Our nature and our instinct are to preserve our culture and protect our traditions.

There was a time when old Guernsey families each had their family home. Our lanes and fields, even rocks and buildings are named after our forebears. Whole tracts of land were owned by one family, including cousins and several generations. This did not make us 'landed gentry', because we have no aristocratic system. But we worked our own soil, and with a strong sense of place.

My family came to live at Solidor, in the Vale, after the Second World War. Solidor was built by my great-grandfather James Heaume. Here, with his wife, Henrietta Domaille, called Harriet, he brought up his family of two sons and four daughters. Of the six children, only two married and had children. And so we arrived at Solidor to a house lived in by a great-uncle and two great-aunts, all single.

Through the blossomy orchard, scattered with clucking red hens, I entered the house for the first time. This was where my grandmother had been brought up. It seemed towering and dark at the back, sunny in the front. We were to have the left wing and ground floor of the main house. Our great-uncle and aunts retained the right wing and remaining floors of their Victorian home.

There was a small conservatory for each wing. Inside the house we found large, high-ceilinged rooms, one with just a piano. But there were views over the Vale pond and meadow. At first everything seemed gloomy and unfamiliar.

But once outside again, the orchard smelt of geraniums and redcurrants. There were stone stables, a pigsty, a henhouse, a washhouse, coal and bicycle sheds. The outside lavatory was covered with Virginia Creeper and the stable walls with pear trees. Further on were greenhouses

14

and, up a small hill, was a thumping generator and slowly turning windmill.

There was a cottage at the end of the property where my father had been born but was then rented out to a Guernsey couple. Our nearest neighbours were cousins who kept bees. They had a stream at the end of their garden which flowed into the Vale Pond. It was called a *douit*, they told us, and we must never go near it. But my brother and I used to lie on its bank with sticks, pretending to fish. We'd collect tadpoles and watch them grow into frogs.

Once we had moved in we gradually explored the rest of the house. In time our family grew from three to five children. Now, I often wonder what our noisy invasion must have been like to those reserved, genteel people, happier speaking Guernsey-French patois than English.

Up in the sprawling attic you could see the ancient Vale Church and my great-aunt's land, which she later sold to the Church and where the Rectory is now built. There was a row of cottages alongside, once belonging to the Domailles including the feudal court-house of Le Fief St Michel. I remember going with aunt Elise to collect her *rentes*. Long ago the family owned a shipyard with land stretching all around La Garenne. There was another, at St. Sampson's harbour. One of the oldest cemeteries is named after them. The Domailles seemed to own much of the land and houses all around the Vale Church. Perhaps they lived in isolated splendour when the Clos du Valle was cut off from the rest of Guernsey? I used to wonder if they were descendants of the Benedictine monks (Doms) who travelled from Mont St Michel in Normandy. There was a priory on the Vale Church hill. Were the Domailles descended from the 'Doms' of the 'isle', or even 'aisle' meaning sanctuary?

Great aunt Elise also had land and greenhouses opposite Solidor which she worked by herself. Later she built a bungalow there. Great uncle Alfred had fields at Chouet and land at Mares Pellées.

One day, when my great-uncle and aunts were out, my brother and I crept upstairs to mooch about, way out of bounds. The stairs had dark mahogany banisters and went up two flights. Great aunt Lil's room was light and airy, with a long, lace-curtained window looking out over the orchard. There were two bookcases and cupboards set into the walls. I took out one of the books. It was called *Eric, or Little by Little*. On a marble-topped table were a white jug, bowl and yellow soap. Aunty Lil's

Yvonne and baby Elizabeth

Solidor, the family home

room was that of a little nun, sparse and clean. She was a gentle soul and would offer us a 'sugar', a Guernsey sweet, every time we went to see her. When I go to Normandy it's as though I still see her: a slight figure with dark hair, centre-parted and a neat bun at the nape of her neck. She always wore black, with a flowered pinafore over her day clothes.

But great-uncle Alfred's room had a magnificent solid mahogany wardrobe. He, too, had cupboards set in the wall but either side of a pretty, tiled fireplace. Above the fireplace was a large gilt mirror, on either end of the mantelpiece sat two porcelain black and white dogs. His bed was a magnificent, mahogany fourposter. Two oil paintings, in gilt frames, dominated the walls. They were landscapes, with colours of yellow ochre and pale blue sky.

In the bay window, overlooking the meadow, stood a dark wood dressing table with three mirrors. Silver-backed brushes were placed carefully on one side. His windows were also dressed with long lace curtains, and, like all the house, had green, wooden Venetian blinds. On a pedestal table was the family Bible, pages edged with gold leaf. On the flimsy front page births, marriages and deaths of the entire family were entered carefully in brown ink. This, I thought, is a gentleman's room.

We crept out onto the landing where another heavy mahogany 'press' stood. This held all the linens and handmade lace cloths bequeathed to them by their own parents and grandparents.

Then, into great-aunt Elise's room: the smallest of the three, with a narrow single bed and, on the wall, a picture of a white-robed angel holding an arum lily. Along another wall was her dressing table, and a cupboard holding silk dresses and fine hats. We quietly opened drawers and found sparkling jewellery which Aunt Elise hardly ever wore. A comfortable commode turned into a chair. At the front facing window was another, cushioned, chair. This was where aunt surveyed the world and knew everything that was going on.

Up in the echoing attic, there were three empty rooms, the length and width of the house, and a separate boxroom. A Singer sewing machine stood near the window. On the floors were drying haricot beans. From here you could see L'Islet beach, fields and the meadow and hear not a sound.

Finishing our illicit mission, we slid down the polished banisters, landing in the hall. The entrance porch was tiled, green and white . A china *jardinière* held an aspidistra. High above a bell on a metal scroll could be clanged if you pulled a handle outside the front door.

Downstairs, the formal sitting room, never used, had long bay windows and, again, a fireplace topped by a gold framed mirror. On a polished table was an ornate gold clock, covered with an oval glass dome.

Their kitchen had a board on the wall, with several bells on and numbers, which we thought must have been for servants at one time. There was a picture of great-grandfather Heaume and one of his dalmation dogs ("He was wicked, that one") and another, of a stern Queen Victoria, wearing a lace cap and looking much like our great-grandmother had. The kitchen was warm with its new Aga. The table was scrubbed, with a bench either side.

There was another small parlour, with a table covered with a brown cloth. In the Summer the table sported a glass bowl with a curved double rim. It was filled with vinegar to catch flies. It was here our great-uncle and aunts entertained. The fire was lit at four o'clock every day. They always spoke patois to each other and to my father.

Many years later, in great-aunt Lil's quiet room, I changed into my wedding dress. I used her Cheval mirror to adjust my veil. She had died long ago. As I walked downstairs, holding on to the mahogany banister, great-aunt Elise and great-uncle Alfred waited for me in the hall. (They never went to weddings.) They wished me luck and opened the front door (rarely done). Out I went, down the clean white steps and yellow gravel path, into the bridal car where my father waited. As we drove forward I glanced back to say goodbye to Solidor. I never lived there again.

Now, like so many Guernsey family homes, Solidor and all its land and property, even the cottage where my father was born, has passed out of Heaume and Domaille hands.

Solidor is still a fine house and looks well cared for. But all around the house has changed, the road in front, where we used to stroll across, is unrecognisable. The meadow is now a wildlife preserve. Our bee keeping cousins have long gone.

Never mind. Guernsey people have rich memories. Each of us has our own unique family story that can never be taken away. And the rest, as they say, is history.

3 Shopping

So we are going to have a new supermarket? Will the little shops cope? It is the 1940s and we have gone to live with our great-uncle and aunt. There were three shops nearby: Luff's, run by Mrs Johns, Rihoy's, guarded by Mrs Rihoy and Lowe's, a family shop, at the Brave crossroads. We can walk to all of them.

My great-aunt put on her second-best hat, and, shopping basket over her arm, we went to Luff's. On the floor were sacks of yellow lentils, sugar and soda crystals. Mrs Johns sliced a hunk of cheese on a marble slab with a cheesewire. Then, she put a ham next to a steel wheel, sharp as a guillotine, sliced it, then some bacon.

Each item was wrapped individually in greaseproof paper, placed in my great-aunt's basket and the price written down in pencil on a list. This was added up and the total announced. From a jar on a shelf Mrs Johns trowelled Guernsey sweets, my great-aunt's favourites, into a paper cone. She weighed them, then twisted them in securely. After adding the cost, a final total and, as well as the money, Mrs Johns took out the stamps from my great-aunt's ration book.

We walked home, past the cottages and the Vale Mission. Home, and the cheese, ham and bacon were put into my great-aunt's safe: a small larder with a mesh door. When Mr Domaille, the milkman, came with his milk churns on a barrow, she placed her filled milk jug on the stone floor of the kitchen.

They grew cucumbers and haricot beans in the tomato greenhouses. The haricot beans were dried on the attic floor. Onions hung in strings from the rafters. Carrots were stored in boxes of sand; green cooking apples were covered in sacking and placed on dark shelves. They lasted all winter. The pig sty was empty now, and the horses and traps were gone. But the stables remained for packing tomatoes, a coal shed, a wash-house and a roost for the hens.

Great-uncle Alf, in his dark brown Trilby, always whistling 'The Blue Danube', tended land at Les Mares Pellées. Once he grew too many cauliflowers and had a glut. Rather than sell them he piled them high on

19

a table with a notice: 'Free. Help yourself'. Nobody did. Ah, but they're a proud lot down Les Mares Pellées!

Mary Bréhaut and Yvonne, 1947

Each Saturday morning my sister went to Town to buy our evening feed of shellfish. On the bus, visitors recoiled as three or four live lobsters' antennae waved at them from her bag. Once she bought two dozen lady crabs; her paper carrier bag burst and the crabs escaped all over the High Street. Visitors ran away terrified. My sister, diving between people's legs, managed to find them all, and on the bus home carried them bundled up in her skirt. "I didn't lose one, Mum," she said, proudly. And she hadn't.

As well as growing, our business was store-packing tomatoes and flowers for customers, then transporting them to the White Rock for shipment to the mainland. In June, when the women workers heard "Mackerel, Mackerel" shouted from the road, my father let them stop work and rush outside to buy their fish. The fresh catch was driven by the fishermen house-to-house in the back of a van. Those who lived nearest popped home to put their fish away. They'd have a mackerel supper with new potatoes and buttered garden peas.

On the two best ormering tides, the men brought their ormering hooks to work. At the right moment, they, and my father ('the boss') all disappeared for the day. They'd finish up at The Houmet du Nord or L'Ancresse Lodge for a pint or two and a count of their catch. Often they had panniers filled with several dozens.

We children were skilled at picking lady and spider crabs, chancres and lobsters. A skill useful to this day when dining at Christies and Le Frégate.

One day, planned for weeks, my great-aunt and I went to Keyhos, in Town, for a new hat. Her hair was newly coiffed, and she wore her very best clothes (silk blouse, ankle-length skirt and coat), pearl necklace, diamond brooch. We sallied forth. Keyhos had a lift to the hat department. When the doors parted my great-aunt sailed out. The assistant immediately found her a chair. Then she brought several hats to her for approval. She served no one else until my great-aunt had, aided with handheld mirrors, decided on a purchase. No money exchanged hands. Later a discreet bill arrived by post.

Afterwards my great-aunt decided we'd go to Le Noury's for afternoon tea. We ordered home-made cream cakes, served on filigree doilies and white china. In the Arcade we bought coffee beans from the Analytical Tea Company, the mouth-watering aroma lingering all around. Carrying her hat-box and coffee, well pleased, my great-aunt and I took a taxi home.

But we usually walked or cycled to the Bridge. My mother, Mary Bréhaut, went to the sisters' Johns wool shop. She chose her wool, buying just a few ounces at a time. Rationing points were needed for clothes. My mother bought us matching blue coats and poke bonnets. Then nothing for herself for many months after that.

Thursday was early closing day. This was the day of *Visite*, of friends and relatives, of home-baked cakes and scones. The men sat on chairs on L'Islet Common, telling each other yarns, bikes leaning on the walls. Or they'd be in their boats, fishing with crab pots, or shooting rabbits, or playing golf. Monday and Tuesday were laundry days. We had meals made from Sunday's roast: cold meat or shepherd's pie. Wednesday was baking day and perhaps, a meaty, vegetable soup. Friday was shopping at the Town Market for meat, poultry and fish. Saturday afternoon was Town, to see and be seen.

Sunday was the day of rest, Church, seeing friends, men's clubs and the North Social. Sometimes we'd go to our Sunday beach, Pembroke, and get a tea basket. This was a tomato chip basket holding proper cups and saucers, teapot, sugar bowl and milk jug. When you took it back your deposit was returned.

Luff's, Rihoy's and Lowe's have all gone now. Lowe's was the largest, most modern and last to go. There were no traffic lights at the crossroads then. The shop had a stone path, over a *douit*, with a lavender border that we stopped at to pick and smell on the way home.

Opposite Lowe's was Stafford-Allan's meadow, the wall bordered with tall trees. No bungalows then. In between the trees we could see horses grazing in the field. We'd park our bikes and call them over, giving them apples. My great-aunt would be baffled by the choice in supermarkets. In her day you only bought what you could carry home and eat within days.

Still, Guernsey's rich soil and the yield from her abundant green sea haven't gone. Nor its islanders who wouldn't live anywhere else in the world.

4 "Coming for a Dip?"

June 2003

"Coming for a dip?" our friends would ask. And off we would go from morning until evening. Since all our parents worked in the greenhouses and packing sheds, at the height of the summer, children had to find their own fun. And we did. In families of five or six, the older children looked after the young ones.

Sandwiches were of freshly caught crab, and tomatoes taken from the over-ripe pile in the packing shed (sweet and juicy). Then, with a packet of Smiths crisps from Mrs Rihoy's corner shop and a bottle of pop, off we went.

We never took buckets and spades and never called the beach 'the seaside' – that was for visitors. There were no toilets or kiosks. Our seaweed was *vraic* and only visitors (not known then as 'tourists') took deckchairs and the like to sit in the sun. We used to watch them as we sunned ourselves on our favourite smooth rocks. Ah, the poor English! Didn't they know everything would get full of sand? And what was the point of being on the beach if you put up parasols and sat on blankets? Anyway, we were closer to the sea for a dip.

As the tide went out we followed it down, shifting our base to little islands of boulders or the small piers that became exposed at low water. If you wanted to fish you took your fishing line, complete with hook and metal sinker. The older ones dug for sandworms for bait but we started with limpets for fishing in the deep rockpools.

The gulleys around the Dolly Rock were the best place for cabot and rockfish. After patiently waiting, lying in the sun, I loved to see a dark fish silently poke its head out of its shadowy hiding place. As it eyed the bait, I would hold my breath. Would it open its mouth and take the morsel? Yes! My line wriggled, the fish was caught! There it lay, wet and flapping on the hot boulder. But I unhooked it and let it go back. Even the cats wouldn't eat cabot.

Under the piers, further out, the boys caught octopus, turning their heads inside out to kill them, black ink spurting over you if you were too close. Once I had one thrown at me and its tentacles clung to my leg.

They had to cut it off me with a penknife, bit by bit, saving it all for bait later on. In their boats and further out the boys used their hooks and landed conger eels. There were ormers at ormering tide. Later some of the boys started scuba diving, becoming expert at deeper sea fishing.

There was always one or two of the gang already down at Les Amarreurs. Usually the boys had already had a swim. We'd spread our towels to bag a space, always using the same place. This went on from early April until well into September.

Great-grandmother Carré, Petit Bot

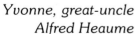

Yvonne, great-uncle Alfred Heaume

The whole beach was ours, and the bays around it. You could see L'Islet, Rousse, Ladies Bay and Chouet from Les Amarreurs. At very low tide, when the sea disappeared into the horizon we could see people paddling and fishing and little white boats on their sides for miles around us. As the seagulls called overhead and we breathed in the salty sea breeze it was as though our entire world surrounded us. We had our very own blue lagoon, all to ourselves.

Brown as berries, we splashed in the sandy-green pools, teaming with shrimps and darting fish. Diving under water with my eyes open in the warm sandy sea, I almost felt like a fish. We'd run as far as we could over pebbles and shingle, climbing over rocks until we came to the pools we thought belonged to us. Here we would dive and swim. Sometimes the boys rowed out to rocks further out, then they'd head back and we'd have our food. We didn't call it 'lunch' or a 'picnic' and wouldn't have dreamt of buying a picnic basket. There wasn't money for that, anyway.

Munching our sandwiches, shivering, since we had swum all morning, we observed the scene around us. You couldn't go back home with a dry towel. It was a sign of how many dips you'd had if your towel was sopping wet.

It didn't matter if the weather was cold and the sea rough. We would still jump off the Big Pier, letting the strong tide carry us, riding the surf and undercurrents. We knew where the best shelter was and how to get out of the wind. If it rained, well, you were wet anyway!

The beaches in the South, Petit Bot, Moulin Huet, Saints and Portelet were all somewhere to visit as an occasion. When my great uncle Alfred took my brother and me to Moulin Huet we wore our best clothes and uncle Alfred hired a chauffered car for the day. This day we did have lunch at the Moulin Huet tearoom and it was very formal. A wasp stung my ankle and I didn't dare tell my uncle.

My husband's maternal great-grandmother visited Petit Bot in full afternoon dress. The southern bays were thought of as beautiful but not for everyday visits. The closest we got to this grandness in the north were L'Ancresse and Pembroke.

On Sundays, my parents' day off, our family went to the middle rocks at L'Ancresse. My father helped us to shrimp and my mother came down with the latest baby and brought food. It was a real outing. The Pembroke bus was always full to standing with visitors, often with a spare bus following behind.

Sometimes my father took us fishing off Herm, in his friends' boat moored at Bordeaux. The Bordeaux moorings, like the Hockey family's, are still highly prized and passed down for generations.

But usually we were found at Les Amarreurs. As the sun lowered into evening the sea changed colour. On a still day, safe on our warm boulders, a violet sea enveloped us, stealing forward with soft rippling waves. This was my favourite time. A last swim in a swirling oncoming tide. The visitors had long ago packed up and gone. The beach was ours again, cooling and bathed in a soft light. Sunburned limbs were soothed with saltwater, washing sand from our feet.

Our bikes waited on the top of the beach, unlocked and in a heap just as we had thrown them. As we peddled home, hungry and tired, we called out to each other, saying we would meet again next day.

There might have been another way, some would say a better way, but this way of life was all we needed. Needing adults to entertain us? Bored? In danger? It never entered our minds.

5 Mystical Les Amarreurs

L' Ancresse Common was our playground. The beaches were for adventures.

One day, long ago, our gang's older boys decided we'd walk through the lanes to Bordeaux. Then we'd scramble over the rocks, all along the edge of the shore until we reached L'Islet, then home. In other words, walk the entire northern end of Guernsey.

We set off along the gravelly shore, admiring Herm, Jethou and Sark, asleep in the warm sun. They were so close to Bordeaux we thought we could swim to them without effort.

A climb up some sandy turf, past sheltered Les Miellettes to wild, deserted Fort Doyle. Then onward, slipping on wet boulders, clinging to grey granite. The air was clean and blue. The mailboat chugged slowly by, heading to Les Casquets, leaving a trail of white surf.

Gulls called to us, whirling and diving over our shoulders. We stopped near deep pools, cold and secretive, to catch cabot with our bare hands. We plopped them back, flapping their tails.

Across untamed Fontenelle Bay, all stones, shale and vigorous sea – and on to Fort Le Marchant. We were forbidden to go near it but climbed up it anyway. We played goodies and baddies, then ran to L'Ancresse Bay. Our feet sank to our ankles in the clean, soft sand of L'Ancresse then – into the sea. Waves curved the length of the bay, coming toward us, sunlit to a pale green. The beach seemed endless as we ran over sea-fresh sand to Pembroke, our favourite sunspot. This was our high-days and holidays beach. Our parents would come on Sundays in their best summer clothes with a picnic of crab sandwiches and over-ripe tomatoes, crisps and pop.

Across the springy common to quiet little Jaonneuse. No wind here, just hot sand and the cry of skylarks. Our sandals slipped over the round, white stones. No rubbish tip yet. Still, though, the Chouet Tower. And all around, fields of shiny grass. Here was Uncle Alf's field of cabbages. Seabirds crying, wild flowers fighting for space in the low, grassy hedges: the pure air on our faces, we ran and laughed and played tag up the narrow hill to Chouet Tower. Not allowed, again, to go in. But we did. The boys climbed to the top and called out to us. You could see across the whole of the lower part of Guernsey here, as far as Town.

A hop and a skip, then Chouet beach itself. Not many golfers then, but some of the finest fishing on the island, off the rocky coast. We waded into the sea and hiked across to Ladies' Bay. We passed an oystercatcher's nest, the eggs almost invisible in the curve of speckled stones. The sand was white and dotted with spiky grasses. We skimmed stones in the sea. Some skipped five, six times.

The big pier. Les Amarreurs

Over the shorn grass then to our beloved Les Amarreurs, dear to our hearts. There was the Big Pier and the Dolly Rock. There, our long flat boulders where we sunbathed. Here we made our camp, as we always did. The boys would catch conger eels, octopus and rockfish. We'd get surrounded, on purpose, and show off to the visitors, wading to safety with our clothes piled on top of our heads. On this beach we learnt to swim, dive and row a boat. We could all fish and catch spider crabs. All summer this was ours.

When the tide went out, it went so far that the sea joined the sky, far out on the horizon. There was, and is, something almost mystically special about Les Amarreurs. This is the Vale's best-kept secret place. This was, and still is, a paradise.

You can see all of the Grand Havre from Les Amarreurs: L'Islet, the Picquerel (another wonderful fishing spot) and Rousse; the haunting Vale Church, pale in the sun, guarding the Garenne. And in the light and reedy Garenne we found a wild pond with frogspawn, lilies and bulrushes. We'd hide in the gorse and watch rabbits coming out for food.

The Vale Pond was nearby. Mr Quevatre's fine herd of Guernsey cows grazed in the meadow and we'd help with the harvest and milking. It wasn't National Trust land yet, but a shortcut if you'd missed the bus and gone to L'Islet instead of Route Militaire.

On this day we swam until the light faded. We lastly trailed along to tiny L'Islet with its myriad yellow shells, gentle bay and smell of pine. The church bells pealed over the air as we made for home. Past the banks of sweet-smelling allysum, next to the church. On to Pont Allaire. We'd done it. Hungry and tired we ran home and smelt mackerel being fried in butter with sweet tomatoes: supper – with tea and warm bread. Build an airport at Chouet? Never!

6 The Growing Business

June 2002

Guernsey people having to leave the island because they cannot afford to buy a house seems unbelievable to my generation.

Mortgages are always expensive. Our first, semi-detached, little house cost £2,000 and we were hard-put for many years to find the money to repay the bank. Women's earnings were not taken into account. But at least first-time buyer houses were on the market.

We were brought up in our great-uncle's family house, built by his father, and all of my relatives were builders or growers. When my sister and I left school to work in offices in Town, we were the first. My cousin Jean was a wonderful seamstress, employed at Delas in St Peter Port. To us, this post was most adventurous, and very prestigious. We boarded our buses each morning with a sense of leaving behind our safe country parish. Heady stuff.

My great-uncle and father ran the smallholding. There were several greenhouses: the big span, the twin span and the lean-to. My uncle used to save good tomato seeds each season and grow them on between glass plates. We would watch the tiny seedlings grow, then get selected, potted and begin to spread their hairy, green leaves. Each year it was fascinating to see the plants race each other to produce their first yellow flowers and then the tiny, green berries emerged, which would be the tomatoes.

Each greenhouse had a character of its own and the green sward of colour as you entered it, the peppery smell and steamed soil were always new sensations. That was, at the beginning of the season. As the year wore on, the inside of the greenhouses became steamy jungles and the work got harder.

The men and women tied young plants with string, strung them to overhead wires, wound the heads around and trimmed unwanted shoots in between each stem. Then came the dreaded job of fertilising. We all hated this. Each flower, laden with pollen, had to be tapped with 'the fertiliser': the first ones were feathers on bamboo sticks, then sticks with brushes and later a device made with a battery.

30

Sometimes we children watched television after school (black and white of course and only BBC). When we heard intermittent buzzes and the screen flickered with interference, we knew it was Mum with her battery fertilizer. We'd tell her off if there were long gaps between flickers: it meant Mum had been slacking.

The soil had been steam-cleaned in the winter, but now needed to be regularly fed and watered, all by hand. The boilers had to be stoked and kept roaring. They were banked up at night. At the height of the season, the glass was sprayed with white lime to keep out the harsher sun rays. Then the never-ending job of picking the crops swung into action.

Alfred Bréhaut, Mont du Val

My father store-packed for himself and customers. In the morning he would do his round, collecting hundreds of baskets of picked fruit. These would be hand-graded in the packing shed. They were each given their own emblem and packing paper colour – this was the paper that lined the wooden basket. The best were packed with pink or white paper – standard-sized fruit with a nice round shape and orange colour that was just turning red. Their baskets would be stamped with a sun or a star. Smaller, but good fruit had a triangle emblem and white paper. The remaining, poorer fruit was graded yellow with a diamond, green with a square or blue with a circle. The over-ripes, which were already red (and no use for shipping), were ours. We got them free and shared them around family and workers alike.

Once the grading was done, the Guernsey toms were packed in paper-lined chip baskets (with pink paper and so on). They were stamped on the side with their grade sign and then nailed down with wooden boards. Later the nailing was done with a machine and later still the chips became trays covered with paper, with 'Guernsey toms' already printed on and stapled.

The good growers were always known. You would hear: 'Cor, old Mahy, he had a good load – nearly all pink and whites. He's the same, every year. But poor old Eustace. He's never got more than blues. He's a bloney fool!'

At lunchtime, or while waiting for a lorry-load, baskets would be papered in readiness. Overtime in the summer was known as 'doing a quarter'. It took place after supper, between 6 and 8 o'clock. Working in the smaller 'fronts' of the greenhouses was the worst. The worker would be bent almost double and it was the hottest part of the house. People would try to leave this until later in the evening, when they did their 'quarter'.

The lights, the windows at the top of the greenhouse, would need to be opened or closed, depending on humidity and sunshine. A Guernseyman would often interrupt a date with a girl to see to his lights or stoke his boiler. First things first.

When all was ready, the toms were loaded back onto father's lorries - he had three at one time, all ex-Army. He and Charlie would take them to the White Rock for shipping. The Guernsey growers depended on the markets for the price their fruit would get. My father, being a commission agent, had contacts in Covent Garden, Birmingham, Leeds, Sheffield, Manchester and Liverpool. The telephone was always ringing with the latest prices. When the idea of all tomatoes, from any grower, going to one big depot came, the demise of tomato growing began. That, and countries like the Netherlands, subsidising their growers. When the very good, self-employed growers, the true private enterpeneurs, went, so did the horticultural industry.

Winno Bréhaut and Charlie Bohan

Everyone, children included when we were not on the beach, earned money helping with fertilising and bunching the other main crops: freesias, iris and daffodils. The stone-floored packing shed, formerly a stable, was cold and the stems of flowers wet. You would twist six stems, place a nob of cotton wool and secure with a rubber band. It was surprising how many buckets you could fill in an hour. We were paid, in cash, by the bunch. The radio was on and we would munch biscuits. In a busy packing shed you would find lots of chatter and laughter as people exchanged gossip and stories. During breaks, the women would nip home to put the dinner on. The lorries were put to all kinds of use: my father and Charlie went coaling for the vinery boilers and vraicing – getting loads of seaweed for growers' field crops. The work was very hard.

Charlie was from Alderney and had a special trick he could do – hanging upside down by his boots from the packing shed door. We thought this was about the cleverest thing we had ever seen.

At the end of the season the plants had grown so high they were trained over the other side of the path. This is still known as a Guernsey arch. It was time for them to be hauled down and dumped. The soil was cleared ready for sterilizing again. The wooden glasshouses would be painted and repaired. Glass panes replaced. Plenty of work for the carpenters.

Now it was time to look forward to the annual shows, especially our North one. We never took a two-week holiday, just days off here and there. We went to Sark and Herm, but to Jersey only for the Muratti. All of these were special events.

When I met a boy from the Forest, also from a growing family, I learnt how different the parishes in Guernsey were. At the age of 17, I would take the bus to Town and then another which took even longer, to the Forest – way past the airport. The first time I did this I marvelled at the hilly fields, the views to the southern cliffs and the blue sea beyond. Walking along Rue Perrot, to my future in-laws' house, I saw so many wild birds, leafy trees and high hedges. And the fields had dark-brown soil. Up here the hedgerows were fertile and dense. As well as tomatoes, my in-laws grew tall gladioli, coloured orange, white, yellow and deep pink.

After a 6am start, they stopped at 12 for their midday meal, always resting for an hour afterwards. Thursday afternoons were a half-day. They employed a couple of men and a lady to help with the freesia crop. But their land was almost as big as my great-uncle's plot.

Yet, many years later, only one house was permitted to replace the one demolished at Rue Perrot and all the greenhouses. And, even then, no dormer windows were allowed. Four houses have now been built in what was our busy backyard.

Gone are the stables, trees and glasshouses. Gone is the life we led. Only the packing shed is still there, but even that is now a workshop. When the growing industry collapsed, so did our way of life. But all is not lost. Nearly, but not quite. Plant a seed in Guernsey and it will grow. We have near-perfect light, temperature and soil conditions – unique in the whole world. If the finance sector ever crumbles, we will thank God for these precious gifts.

Someone said recently: 'Renovate existing houses, make legislation so that only first-time buyers can own inexpensive property' in their own island. Well said. Young Guernsey people have a right to the island and its extraordinary history of enterprising independence. We are natural importers and exporters, with keen eyes for successful commerce. Before tomatoes, Guernsey had industries like the grape vineries, woollens, fishing and shipbuilding. Aqua Star landed a major prize at the London Boat Show and Guernsey Clematis is a gold medal-winner at the Chelsea Flower Show, exporting worldwide. Guernseymen and women are the island's future.

Fortunately, like our ancestors, we never give up.

7 Eyebrow House

The day begins with the cockerel's cry, echoing through the still morning air. There is a distant crow as his friend responds. Their watch is over. It is six o'clock and all's well. We lie in our beds, listening to our sentinels. We have been waiting for this day.

In the yard outside, Great Aunt Elise pumps water from the well. She's fetched eggs from her lazy hens, who scratch and cluck underneath the apple trees. They flap and fluster their red feathers. Two seagulls sit on the old stable roof, cackling and squabbling over their breakfast of flung bread crusts.

Today is Thursday, the growers' half day off. And our Uncle Jack is coming to take us for a drive in his new car, all the way to Pleinmont. Our shoes are polished, we wear new ribbons and white gloves. At last Uncle Jack arrives, handsome in his tweed suit and Trilby. His fair-haired wife wears the New Look and a soft beret with a spotted brown feather in it. We all squeeze into the black Ford and wave goodbye to Great Aunt Elise. She has changed her clothes from black dress and flowered apron to lace blouse and long pleated skirt. For it is now after lunch and she awaits her friends, for tea and buttered *gâche*.

Uncle Jack decides that we'll drive across the field. We are excited by this adventure. It is a rare treat. We see Saumarez Park, which we know from going each year to the North Show in our father's lorry. What a lot of trees! Then, on through King's Mills with its fine granite houses, covered with wisteria and creeping vines. We are miles from home!

On to La Rue Du Dos D'Ane, 'the donkey's back', turning through the leafy trees forming arches over our heads. We pretend we are in a rabbit warren. The hedges are much higher than in the Vale. Through some gates we see fields unknown to us.

In one, a farmer salutes us as he ploughs the rich earth with two chestnut brown horses. They have jingling brasses and nod their heads as they pull their load. The ploughed furrows are dotted with white gulls and more, streaming behind, in the air. How they call out, anticipating their free meal. The sky is wide and blue. Yellow daffodils wave gently

35

on the hedges in the sea breeze.

Then the little Ford, alone on the lanes, turns again. We are at the reservoir in St Saviour's. Here, we get out and walk. Uncle Jack wants to show us the new dam. It is a marvel: still lake on one side, torrent of rushing water the other. We stand on the long stone bridge. We have to step up to get a good view of the pine trees and then admire the spectacular drop. We shiver with awe.

'The Eyebrow House', Rocquaine

Walking back to the car, we pick posies of primroses. These grow in pale yellow masses, all over the hedges. One day we'll come back and pick great bunches of them and put them into the boxes of daffodils my father packs. The boxes of daffodil, freesia and iris are headed for Covent Garden. We can keep the few pence the primroses make, for our moneybox.

On now, winding down to Pleinmont, as far as we 'northerners' can go. Rocquaine is a wide sweep of sand, secured by its curve of sea wall. Men sit gossiping on the wall. The women are in the tea rooms.

We can see the Cup and Saucer and Uncle Jack says the locals sunbathe beneath the pier there, in the summer. And, he says, families have their own part of the beach. So the Le Couteurs, the Lenfestys and the Robilliards would never dream of taking each other's territory. Portelet is exotic. We are not used to trees and grass growing so close to the beach. They almost touch the sand of the bay. We pretend we are in a foreign land, far away.

The fishing boats bob on the water. Some have families in them, off for a trip. Some are being rowed across the bay, some have people fishing from them. Soon it will be time for the Rocquaine Regatta. We have the North Regatta. It has a funfair by the Weighbridge and competitions on the beach.

I never win anything. Then, Uncle Jack has a surprise. He buys us an ice cream each. We have never tasted ice creams before, not with real cream. Dellarose, peddling his wares on his bicycle up and down the L'Ancresse Road, only sold ices tasting of white lard. And these cream ones have got wafers, not paper wrappers. We take off our gloves, lick our lips and devour every sweet, creamy drop.

It is time to go home. We are going to go all along the coast road. As we head north, we look out of the Ford's back window. There is a house, high on the horizon, with a view over Rocquaine and its sparkling sea and orange setting sun. Who lives there?

Once, it is said – Uncle Jack tells us – Prince Edward and his Wallis Simpson stayed there, a safe house, for a holiday. We stare a bit longer. The safe house, with the funny roof, stares back. And, as we leave, we imagine this majestic coast in winter. In the cold – when the awesome ocean flings its waves high over the sturdy wall: when the pebbles and *vraic* hurl themselves into the boarded windows of the fishermen's cottages, huddled together for safety – what then? When the gales shake the very foundations of this bay, when the storms rage, the mists fall and the fields flood – what happens to this furthest place in Guernsey?

The Eyebrow House keeps watch.

8 *Aunty Lil*

October 2005

Television can be at best inspiring, at worst trite. Two programmes lately were in the first category and made me really think. One was '7-Up' tracing the lives of a group of 'ordinary people' every seven years since they were seven years-old. The other was Rick Stein, travelling through France and admiring regional dishes. He waxed lyrically over *cassoulet* and I couldn't help smiling at what that reminded me of.

Of all the great Aunts that I had, Aunty Lil stayed the most French and the most 'ordinary'. We arrived to live at her family home in 1946. It was a Victorian house built by her father and shared with her brother (great-uncle Alfred and sister, great-aunt Elise). None of them had married. They ran the house, land and horticultural business for themselves.

The Heaumes were descended from the French Huguenots, from the area of La Rochelle. Aunty Lil, a mild mannered and quietly spoken soul, was in charge of the chickens, which roamed freely in the orchard. There was a small hen-house, covered with Rubberoid, where the chickens roosted at night. It was fun to round up the fowls and chase them, squawking, onto the roosts where they slept.

Aunty Lil let us children look for eggs and we found them under the apple trees, in long grass and under the lilac bushes. Sometimes they were still warm. But, again, at times they had lain hidden for too long and were rotten. It was always best to crack them open in a bowl before adding them to others for an omelette. Our aunt had some white china eggs which she put under the bad layers to encourage them to lay. If the bird still didn't lay then she would ring its neck and sit, on a chair in the yard, and pluck it. Feathers would fly everywhere and the hapless bird ended up in a very tasty stew.

I still love to hear hens clucking away as they amble about, pecking at the ground. There was a red-feathered hen which became quite tame and often came into our kitchen. We called her Hettie and she let us pick her up.

We had two pet rabbits as well, a black-haired one called Trixie and a

Aunty Lil, Solidor, 1947

white one, mine, called Ruffles. Aunt Elise complained that Aunty Lil was left too often to clean the hutches and feed the rabbits whilst we were at school.

One day, we came home to empty hutches. We had left the work to Aunty Lil for the last time. There was a delicious aroma coming from the saucepan on her Aga. And this time, it wasn't of chicken.

My father kept crabpots so after a good catch, when she was given several crayfish to cook, Aunty Lil would do the cooking in a large pan on top of the boiler in the outside washhouse. She would split them in two and share the cooked halves with my mother.

And, when Rick Stein enthused about 'cassoulet' in his television programme, the ingredients were almost identical to those of the Guernsey 'Bean Jar'. The Heaumes, like many Guernsey people, kept pigs and grew their own haricot beans.

The Bean Jar was, and is, a tasty rib-sticking casserole that is slow cooked and can feed a large, hungry family. But we certainly never thought of it as a delicacy.

Aunty Lil spoke softly and in Guernsey French patois. She was a kind and gentle lady who always wore black, long-sleeved blouses, long black skirt and black stockings. She wore a flowered apron over the blouse and skirt. Her dark hair was parted in the middle and worn in a chignon at the back. She wasn't a follower of fashion, but always wore modest, good quality clothes that lasted for years.

I still see old women like Aunty Lil in France and other parts of rural Europe. They always remind me of her and the way of life that was lived in the Forties. The Second World War had happened by the time we went to live with our aunts, but the Guernsey traditions had by no means died out yet.

Cool well water was preferred. It was drawn by the pump next to the washhouse where the bicycles were kept. Uncle Alfred went everywhere on his bike, but Aunty Lil walked slowly because she was born with a crooked hip.

I don't recall my aunt ever going away on holiday or even leaving the house and garden. Yet, she kept a map of the world in her kitchen and was very knowledgeable about countries, capital cities and oceans. Her grandfather had been a ship's Captain, from La Grève, Vale, and was drowned at sea along with his two sons. Her grandmother never left her room after that tragedy. At the top of one of the landings, there was a large picture of a boat and its crew in trouble. It was entitled 'For those in peril on the sea' and all the Heaumes remembered their relatives with prayers when they passed that picture.

I didn't ever see Aunty Lil in coat and hat. Aunt Elise did all the shopping, at the corner shop or going by bus to St Peter Port. In their young days they went to Town in the family horse-pulled carriage. The road to the Halfway was bordered on both sides by trees and fields, and there was only one house along the way.

They all remembered the First World War and told us of the young men that they knew who never came back. In those days your parish was your world. Each family, each person, had a place in their parish so that losses like those of war were keenly felt.

Uncle Alfred had pledged to look after his little sister Lil and they were very close. Alfred was also a great benefactor, often helping parishioners to start up their own businesses. The greenhouses and land gave employment to many men and women living nearby. We grew up in the midst of a thriving and busy vinery.

My abiding memory of Aunty Lil is of her sitting quietly in her rocking chair of an evening. She would open up the Aga door and bask in the warm glow of the hot coals. Her two cats sat at her feet. As we children spoke to her she would smile but rarely answer in English. She would offer us a 'sugar' (a sweet) from her hoard of Guernsey sweets kept in a jar.

Aunty Lil had all she wanted. She lived, some might say, an uneventful life. There were no frills or entertainment. It was quite a Spartan existence. But she was content and totally without vanity. I loved her humility, reserve and honourable manner. For such a little lady she left a huge impression and good example. An 'ordinary' life she may have had, but we shall not see her like again.

9   Grandad Bréhaut

March 2005

Guernsey was strange to me when we arrived back in 1946 after being evacuated to the Cotswolds. My parents left the island in 1940 when my elder sister was only four months-old. I was born on May 10th, 1942, in Cheltenham, Gloucestershire. Very soon after that my father, who had joined the Royal Air Force, was posted to India for four years.

I had become used to the Cotswold countryside of rolling golden fields with hedgerows on the horizon and tall leafy trees full of cawing black rooks. At first Guernsey seemed to me to be all and only about the sea. These horizons were a line of blue, and the bays were studded with granite rocks. Fishermen's piers and low grassed common land all but encircled the beach. The pungent smell of leathery *vraic* and the feel of the sand in my shoes were strange to me.

We went to live with my grandparents in La Haize, Vale and my earliest memories are of the walks we took as we played in the lanes around their cottage. Even now the sight and feel of the loose-stone walls mean Guernsey's lanes. The walls were home to families of snails, *colimachaon*, when you turned the stones over– and thick with wall pennywort, shiny green circles bearing spikes of tiny yellow bells that we called 'bread and cheese'. These, and pellitory, with its greyish green and sticky leaves and pink flowers that we played 'tick tack too, the devil's on you' with, bring back the Forties to me. All over the island, these plants are still there: still forever little Guernsey.

White gulls with yellow beaks and searching eyes flew low over our heads, their feet tucked either side of them, neat as the cuttlefish we found on the shoreline. If a gull splattered you, which they often did – and still do – well, we counted that as good luck. It was all part of a walk or a bike ride and we got to know the names of many wildflowers, birds and of the fish in the rockpools. We knew our celandines from our buttercups, our sea bindweed from convolvulus. And we knew when and where the birds would make their nests in spring, and which part of the beach contained pools deep and large enough for rockfish. We dug for our own bait and hooked our own lines as our parents worked in the

Grandad Bréhaut and Edwin, 1916

greenhouses, built houses or fished for a living.

My grandparents stayed in Guernsey during the Occupation and saw many relatives die without them ever seeing their children, grandchildren and great-grandchildren again. My parents, uncles and aunts had managed to keep together in Goucestershire and three of us were born in England.

Edwin Bréhaut, my grandfather, had the gentlest speaking voice of anyone I have ever known: it was a soft voice with a smile in it. He always wore a flat cap, navy Guernsey and grey trousers. He kept pigs and ducks at the bottom of the field which was the back garden. His blue eyes always smiled at me and I, a shy and nervous child, loved him on first sight.

Although they grew tomatoes, I never felt that my grandfather was a natural grower. More of a gardener, he grew roses – lovely sweet smelling yellow ones outside his packing shed where he kept his bike. One end of the packing shed was the outside toilet which I dreaded. The loo seat was one piece of wood with a hole in the middle and I never locked the door for fear of disappearing and nobody knowing what had happened to me.

My husband Tony has indelible memories of an outside lavatory at his aunt and uncle's house at Rocquaine, where, not only did the lavatory not have a flush but the pit underneath was open at the back! It was a bit chilly on windy days, with the gale coming unchecked from the sea. Not only that, the slab of wood had two holes, side by side, so that you could have a companionable chat with another person whilst completing transactions.

Tony also remembers the outside lavatory, again at one end of a shed in the garden, at his family home in Rue Perrot, Forest. As a little boy in the Forties, it was so cold that he used to take with him a lighted candle in its candlestick. This was not so much for light as the warmth it generated.

Grandad rode his bike everywhere and my grandparents never owned a car. His favourite evening haunt was the L'Ancresse Lodge which he frequented with his dog, a large black and white spaniel called Paddy. Paddy resolutely kept himself to himself but followed my grandfather wherever he went.

Edwin's father had been a stonemason and builder. Edwin was brought up in the Castel with his two brothers. One, Frederick, always called Freddie, was killed at Cambrai, France during the First World War.

After marrying my grandmother Adèle, a Heaume, from the Vale, Edwin first lived in Solidor Cottage where my father was born, the first of five children. The lane next to Solidor Cottage is called La Folie which I always liked as a name, and at the top of La Folie is La Haize.

So, as children we walked from Solidor to La Haize and back again all our childhood. And La Haize was handy for getting the Paragon bus at Baugy. That was, if you had missed the green school bus going from L'Ancresse Terminus to Town via Route Militaire, which we often did.

The Bréhauts originated in the Higher Parishes, we were told. And there is a Bréhaut area and Les Bréhauts house still in St Pierre du Bois. But Granddad became a Vale-ite and lived in the parish until he died: peacefully at his own fireside.

Now, as I walk down the lane where we did as children, I can still see the field where Grandad grew potatoes, and remember the fresh smell of the new leaves as they burst out of the dug mounds. Our shoes would get covered with warm dry earth as we carefully manoeuvred our way to the bottom of the garden. I see the pig sty and the stone walls covered still with the shiny green pennywort and I listen out for Grandad's quiet laughter. But now that, of course, has gone for ever.

10 The Greenhouse

February 2006

Island icons? Mine has to be the greenhouse. Each parish in Guernsey has its own family vineries. Some were sprawling, with fields and packing sheds. Some were smallholdings, with three or four greenhouses and maybe a plot of land where owners had built their bungalow.

Even now, everywhere we look, there is evidence of vineries: horticulture and the growers way of life. Sometimes we live in a *clos*, which used to be a vinery. We might still have greenhouses and grow fruit and flowers, but more often now a greenhouse is used to house a variety of other things.

Greenhouses make good sheds, or house a swimming pool or a leisure area – used much as you would a conservatory. People have set up businesses in them. You can see those all over Guernsey. Guernsey people still show great enterprise and ingenuity.

In our youth, though, greenhouses were for growing in and it was a serious business. Our lives revolved around the season and the health of tomato plants. You fitted in with the livelihood of growing tomatoes, and that was that.

Around February and March the January seedlings had been brought on, pricked out (into small pots, ready to be sorted – the weaker ones discarded) and began to show the first signs of green buds and leaves.

This was my favourite time: going in to the Big Span and the Little Span, (two wide greenhouses roofed over as one) and walking up along the paths, taking in the wonderful peppery smell of the freshly watered green leaves. As far as I could see was a lush, living emerald green carpet – newly grown and as near to the hope of spring you could imagine.

Time was you could measure the ongoing season by the height of the tomato plants. Winter into spring brought the yellow flowers, heavy with pollen, aching to be fertilised. After that, the plants, waist high by now, came bunches of small green tomatoes growing bigger every day.

Then the growers' season really swung in as the toms turned red ripe for packing and despatching to the mainland. We store-packed for other growers so our backyard buzzed like a beehive with workmen and lorries.

Jim Domaille, Solidor, 1900

We didn't see much of our parents in the summer. If they weren't picking or watering the tomato plants (by hand with a rubber hose – a heavy and tiring job) they were in the packing sheds. There was feeding of the plants to do, stoking and cleaning the boiler pits. We loved watching the greenhouse hands de-clinkering the boiler. With a rake, they teased out great red-hot chunks of anthracite, dumping them into the pit where they sizzled until cold. If you were idle, you could be handed a fertilising stick (with a feather on the end) and find yourself spending a good hour or two spreading pollen.

We'd 'help' to sort tomatoes by size. The first graders were merely boxes with drawers of different sized holes. Tip the tomato chip basket up and the tomatoes tumbled down to the bottom. The big ones got the best prices, the ones at the bottom the least. Although these were the ones we liked the best: small, sweet and misshapen.

In the packing shed were packets of different coloured paper, thin as tissue, to line the chip baskets before they were nailed down by hand with a hammer. We stole paper and chip lids, making sail boats for the pond.

All my cousins lived close by and we knew no other world than growing. It had its good points: Sunday afternoon strolling around the vinery, noting the plants' growth, comparing crops with others. Everyone was in the same boat.

Our vinery had a lean-to (half a greenhouse, 'leaning' against a wall) where my great-uncle Alfred kept a generator. I still smell the oil from that generator, thumping like a great oily heart with a grey belt going round and round. For here, purple grapes were grown. The picture is of great-uncle Jim Domaille, showing off his prize winning grapes, "Arriving, in Covent Garden, London," my grandmother said, "still with their bloom on."

Grapes were now redundant. Flowers: freesias, carnations and roses were higher up the good-earner list. But my uncle, like many other growers, grew things for the domestic kitchen: grapes, cucumbers, capsicums (peppers), haricot beans, basil and so on.

My father-in-law grew parsley in between his marigolds, lavender and thyme. The Forest soil is brown as chocolate cake and very fertile. I remember my mother-in-law bunching the gladioli they grew. I have never since seen any as sturdy and colourful as they were: rose pink, geranium red and creamy white.

So, the season moved on. High summer we would go to the beach and leave the adults to it. School was out and we became tanned and lithe as fish. Tea would be late evening (never called dinner), especially if the toms had to be ready for shipping next morning.

Breakfast was light and swift, for an early start. And dinner (not lunch), would be dishes like stews and bean jar. There wasn't time to prepare or eat more than one course. Almost always wives helped their husbands.

The weather was always anxiously checked. Very hot sun was no better than a cold day, since the tomatoes would be forced on too quickly – too ripe for shipping. When that happened, the greenhouses were sprayed with white lime to act as shade.

Fog was dreaded or stormy weather, since the boats couldn't trade between the mainland and Guernsey. There was always a constant anxiety until the end of August, when the tomato crop finished.

Then it was the North Show: to see other people's efforts in the fruit and vegetable tent; a chat with the farmers as they proudly showed their best animals. The Battle of Flowers – then summer was over.

Now began the hauling down of the spent plants, withered and stringy. Next, the soil would be cleaned by the steam-boilers, so the men still had much work to do.

When I pass collapsing greenhouses, looking like bad teeth in what was once Guernsey's bright and confident smile, I grieve. Not for the bad times, of course – the back breaking work and all the worries. But, that our childhood playgrounds have disappeared, and with them the customs of our great and grandparents.

I have been watching the TV programme 'Who do you think you are?' Well, Guernsey people have the great privilege of knowing where family houses were built. We can trace family names, even knowing which parish we came from.

When I see a greenhouse, I can feel the warmth of the sun as we played as children. I can hear my great-aunt Elise call my uncle Alfred for his dinner. For, for us, greenhouses were not just for growing tomatoes in, they were our whole way of life. And now, that's all gone.

11 Precious Land

January 2004

So we have the Rural Area Plan, before us. The planned landscape of Guernsey for many years to come.

How precious our land is, and how little we have to squander. Although on our walks through the lanes on hills in Castel and St Andrew's, Torteval and St Saviour's we see the gentle sloping fields, bordered with hedgerows with hardly a house in sight, we know that this is all we have. In Spring the wild-flowered banks, made glorious by yellow daffodils, primroses and fragile violet are of life-enhancing beauty. A small furrowed field, dotted with sitting white gulls, ends with a blue strip of sparkling sea. The view from Jerbourg over the sea to Herm, Sark, all the Channel Islands and France must be unbeatable in Europe. How pretty Guernsey can be, but how vulnerable.

The scores of people, societies and companies submitting their thoughts to the Planning Inquiry all want to guard their stake in Guernsey. Each one of us, right now, is responsible for our future, our heritage and for what we leave to our children and grandchildren.

Our ancestors didn't always get it right. Whole tracts of land, bequeathed to them by their more careful parents and great-grandparents were sold off, piecemeal, for profit. But the money got spent and so generations have been left with nothing. Sometimes family houses were given away, also land, as wedding presents and dowries. With families of eight or nine children, inheritances soon dwindled.

Even large families petered out. After two world wars, not everyone married, not everyone had sons. So names, branches of a family, ended. A few, like the Careys, Doreys and de Saumarez got it right.

Our family home (and several others) was built by my great-grandfather, Alfred Heaume. One of his workers was, splendidly, called Venus De La Mare. He rose at six o clock each day and walked from St Peter's to the Vale. He pencilled his name on a joist in our attic: 'Venus De La Mare, 1890', a proud and happy man.

Today, once more, financial gain at the cost of losing land threatens Guernsey. We can never get our growing community back again, nor our grandparents, great uncles and aunts. How I miss them. How I wish I could go again to the farmhouse kitchens and the quiet sitting rooms where people had afternoon naps and chickens clucked outside.

Great-great-grandfather Heaume (centre)

Every Sunday my in-laws went to Aunty Milly and Uncle Nick's in Torteval. Whilst the men swapped yarns over a whisky or two, the women caught up with all the news. By four they were home, for an evening meal, prepared in the morning. Their routine never changed. But they are all gone now, their houses and land sold to strangers.

No, we can't all have a sea view. Yet all we want, at least, is a little bit of garden, or patio or terrace. Just somewhere to sit in the sun, to spend a time of peace and quiet to ourselves. There is a Jewish saying "Every man has the right to sit under his own vine without fear of terrorism." So, even if the vine be bought from the market garden and the seat be very small, we have a right to it. France, Spain and New Zealand offer our people their space and warmth. And they'll have enough money left to live a decent quality of life. Guernsey is losing her people by the boatload.

In one Vale road, in nine separate households, lived, for many years, members all from the same family, a stone's throw from the family house. Amongst them were three sisters and a brother, although they rarely met socially. Apples, in Guernsey, then, didn't fall far from the tree.

In Folie Lane, we knew everyone, and in the cottages along Route Militaire, near the Vale Church. We walked and cycled everywhere, saying hello to people in their gardens, going to Sparke's shop. We knew where the wicked dog was, and which house to hurry by. They knew our business, we knew theirs.

To live in a parish six miles away was thought most strange. When I married and first moved to the Forest, my mother used to shout down the telephone. When I asked why, she said it was a bit like making a trunk call. True.

Yet, it was different. The houses were further apart. You went by bus to Portelet and Rocquaine. There was more farming in the High Parishes, more crops in fields. The Forest and St Peter-in-the-wood were not called that for nothing. The land is rich and south facing. In the northern Vale, our soil was sandy so we built more greenhouses and made the soil good ourselves. I remember sacks of hoof and horn and blood and bone kept in our sheds.

Now, driving from south to the north, as soon as I reach the Friquet, things change. The sky is wider and lighter, the wind lessens and I know I am coming home. Driving along Bulwer Avenue or Grande Maison road, you soon reach the Bridge. There, always, are true Guernsey people. People are as they were, unchanged and unchangeable. Will a new St Sampson's harbour and development of Leale's yard change everything? Pray not.

As children we played in the Vale Church cemetery. It wasn't at all scary, but quiet, sunlit and safe. We read the tombstones of families that rest in peace there. Sometimes we'd straighten up the flowers or put more water in a vase. Now I try to find my great uncles and aunts but there are no headstones and they are lost to me.

All there is now are the houses they lived in, memories of their island life, and with those, our own roots. Are we the last generation to cherish our island? If, after all, Guernsey people sell houses and their land for plots their own people can't afford, let finance dominate us, our ancient culture will go. Just like our ancestors, we will have gained in the short term and left very little for the others.

Our resourcefulness is renowned. So is our stubbornness. There are a few strong, wise people trying to look after our heritage, future and our environment. Soon there will be island-wide elections. This time there's no room for political self-seeking. This time we have to get it right.

50

12 Make Believe

October 2004

Half-term and many families have gone away for a week. The places include Rome, Spain, London, France, Jersey and England. Lucky children: when we were young, these were places we would not have gone to, even as a main holiday.

Last summer families took two weeks in Australia, New Zealand, South Africa and the USA. People have weddings now in Malaysia, Barbados and the Mediterranean.

I look after my grandchildren and think how different their lives are to ours, in the Forties and Fifties. We go to Aladdin's Cave where the shelves are stocked with Barbie dolls, Barbie clothes even Barbie cars. Children don't even have to wait for Christmas now, it seems, or their birthdays. We only had toys bought for us on those two occasions.

When I was two we had been evacuated to the Cotswolds. My father was serving in India and my mother had to make do, as did everyone in those days. One Christmas my mother's brother-in-law made cots for my sister and I. They were wooden, painted yellow inside and pink outside. My mother made mattresses, pillows and sheets and rag dolls to go with the cots. We played with these things for hours, quite content. And we went on long walks with my mother in the Cotswold lanes. When we returned to Guernsey, we did the same thing.

An outing was simply walking the lanes to the beach. In the Winter we wrapped up warm. We'd collect leaves to press in a book and shells to decorate glass jars.

My brother had a Dinky car collection, which he used to line up like a long train. Woe betide you if you stepped on one of them or knocked over a toy lorry. It was difficult not to, since his 'train' went through the kitchen and into the lounge.

My elder sister and I loved paper dolls. These were cardboard cut out 'girls' and 'boys'. Our favourites were 'Grace' and 'Fred' and we had a large box of cut-out clothes for them. We made them go to parties and visit friends, lost in a make-believe world.

One day Fred's head fell off and we tried to stick it back on. We

51

The Carré children at Hauteville, 1911

went to Creasey's toy shop, to find another book with a 'Fred' in it. There was one but the colours were more faded. So we left 'Fred' in the shop and made do with the original one, now a bit wonky.

My brother loved making houses with his rubber bricks, I think they were called 'Mini-Bricks'. It was a very constructive game and we learnt how walls were made, and how to fit windows. At school we like skipping and playing jacks. The boys played conkers and had stamp collections. We bought stamps at Bakers Bazaar and at Wilson's in Smith Street.

Out of doors we would swim, walk and cycle everywhere. There was far less traffic, so we could be out all day, roaming all over the place, wherever we wanted to. One day our little gang trespassed over people's back gardens. In the Folie Lane, we rambled from Route Militaire to opposite the Quevatre family houses. At the top of the small quarry there was a copse. Branch by branch, leafy twig by leafy twig, we built a den. We wove the branches and twigs, making three sides. Low hanging trees made the roof. We called our den 'Goldy Green', because of the colour of the leaves. We thought one of our cousins was very brave because her headteacher at the time was Miss Quevatre, and we were on her land.

Next day, we took packets of biscuits, scrumped some apples and had a picnic in 'Goldy Green'. Huddled together, we munched away, all the while wondering if we would get discovered. We never did.

When my mother-in-law was a little girl she had the privileged life of the comfortably off. Her dolls and prams were almost as good as a real baby's. They had a summer house, picnics, beach parties and rides with carriage and horse. Her childhood was just before the First World War, a time of great elegance and charm. Guernsey must have been quite magical then.

Now, I drive my grandchildren to the shops on roads that are crowded with cars, drivers not seeming to know the highway code. People pull out of yellow lines without looking. Pedestrians stroll in front of the car without looking either to right nor left.

Buying toys and games for the children, I marvel at the choice. There are all kinds of pens and painting sets. The children love stickers and there are endless choices of butterflies, horses, hearts and flowers. They remind me of the scraps we used to collect in tins. Again, we bought these at Bakers Bazaar. My favourites were the chubby pink angels, gazing heaven-wards.

We would take our tins of scraps to school to do "swaps". If you had two of one you could swap it for something someone else had two of. And we liked 'transfers', which you put over your hand and wet it. The fun was peeling of the paper to see the brightly coloured transfer on your hand. It was a shame to wash it off, and sometimes we didn't, for days.

We treasured our toys and kept them sometimes for years. They weren't going to be replaced. Before plastic had come on to the market nothing was plentiful. Things like Meccano were made of metal, and would be added to, not thrown away. And a box of wooden bricks would be passed down, generation to generation. Choice was limited. But that didn't stop our enjoyment one bit.

I still haven't been to Australia, New Zealand or America. No doubt my grandchildren will tell me all about them one day. They'll probably tell me that they hopped over there, "You know, Gran – for half-term".

13 Vale School

August 2001

St Martin's and Amherst schools have existed for a hundred years. My great-grandfather, Alfred Bréhaut, was a stonemason who helped to build St Martin's School. He took a photograph showing his workmen holding the tools of the trade they specialised in. We travelled from Folie Lane to the Vale School. I first went to school by tricycle. All our friends walked or cycled to school every day and we came home for 'dinner'. We carried leather satchels holding our wooden pencil cases, books and jam sandwiches. There was a water fountain in the playground if you got thirsty. Near it were fragrant sweet peas spilling over the wall from next door's garden. The journey to school took us past low stone walls, the Quevatre's barking bulldog and the hedgehog man. Mr Davenport had some greenhouses in Folie Lane. One day he called us over and showed us a mother hedgehog with three tiny baby hedgehogs nestling under brambles and ferns.

We'd go to La Haize, where our grandparents lived, and visit them on the way home. Then to Baubigny crossroads (no filter) and past a small, ruined cottage. It has gone now. There was no Maison Maritaine, but a fine house and open fields. Facing us was the big hill. We struggled up it – but free-wheeled down, racing our friends, with the wind in our faces.

At the Vale Infants' School, in 1947, we began our lessons rolling plasticine into 'snakes', then shapes of letters. These we pressed onto individual cardboard. The classroom was warm. The teacher wrote with white chalk onto a blackboard, supported by a tripod. In the spring, tadpoles in a jar and wildflowers stood on the window sills.

Miss Fry was the headmistress. We were told she had a stick, which she used on naughty children. One day I, aged six, was summoned to her classroom. "Where had I parked my tricycle?", she asked me.

"Near the gate," I said.

"You are supposed to use the bicycle shed. Where is it?" she said. The older children started giggling. "At the top," I said (meaning at the top of the playground).

55

"The top. On top of the school roof?", she asked. More laughter. I was struck dumb at this.

"Go and stand in the corner," she said, "until you can tell me where the bicycle shed is." Terrified, I wondered if the stick was about to come out of her desk. After about a quarter of an hour, which seemed like all morning, Miss Fry questioned me again. This time I managed to please her. But I never took my tricycle to school again.

In Miss Honey's class I learned to write. On a lined page, you took your pencil from top to bottom, and carefully drew a circle to the right. You'd made a 'b'. If you put the circle on the other side you had 'd'. When you dropped your pencil below the ruled line, you'd got 'p'. I thought this was wonderful! Now I made sense of our first reading books. There were the very same shapes! I was reading!

After that, the arrival of the library box from England was a treasured treat. Oh, the fun of selecting a book, with shiny covers. It went straight into my satchel to take home. When I got to Miss Fry's class, she wasn't so bad. Books had now become my firm friends.

At playtime we had to queue for scalding-hot Horlicks, which burnt your tongue. This came from a steamy urn and was to build us up after years of rationing. We had 'PT' as well, to get us fit.

But I loved my nature book. One side blank, the other lined. We'd go for walks with our teacher in the lanes around the Vale School, as far sometimes as the Vale Mill. We'd collect leaves, flowers and berries. On our return we would draw them and write down their details.

The boys wore short trousers, shirts, ties and pullovers. The girls wore mostly dresses and knitted cardigans, with our hair in plaits and ribbons. Some children were much poorer than others. There was no uniform, so we could tell who was better off. One boy lived with his large family on a boat in St Sampson's harbour. Another girl lived in rooms next to a noisy pub at the North Side. We thought this was very glamorous indeed. She was very popular.

Sometimes we had birthday parties, always held in our own homes. We had paste sandwiches, home-made cakes, jelly and custard. We played musical chairs and blind man's bluff, which I hated. You took a present, but didn't expect anything back except, perhaps, a piece of cake. Bigger parties, like the RAF ex-servicemen's Christmas party for children, were held at the Royal Hotel. Ralph O'Toole would do conjuring tricks and ventriloquism. You had to go up when your name was called and get a present from Father Christmas. My favourite one was 'Jack and Jill' by Louisa M. Alcott. Later, when we had swimming lessons, we went to Havelet, in St Peter Port. Our swimming teacher, well wrapped up at the poolside, urged us on in freezing water. My sister could do triple somersaults off the diving board, swam for the island against Jersey and took part in the floodlit swimming galas held at Havelet each year. I could swim, but diving was beyond me.

St Martin's School, 1901

When the time came to leave the Vale School our headmaster, Roy Carré, told us at our last assembly: "All your lives you will find competition. At your next school and, if you go to university, whatever you do, you will always be judged by what you have achieved. All your lives you must do your best, work hard and do what it takes to make the life you want. Be true to yourself, and don't be discouraged."

I didn't know my great-grandfather. But, a hundred years ago, he used his skilled work on a fine school. St Martin's is, proudly, still here.

14 Battle of Flowers

August 2002

This year we will have our Horticultural Shows to look forward to. How we missed them last year, that time of turmoil and worry. But, in the Forties we went, as we always did, to the North Show. The glorious summer is over. The tomato growers' and farmers' crops are gathered. Swimming, fishing and sunning ourselves will soon be only a memory. We get ready for the Battle of Flowers.

Our mother has whitened our sandals with Meltonian cream. Five pairs of assorted sizes dry on the greenhouse. It is a sunny day and we are all dressed in our summer best. Mum wears a floral cotton frock, Dad is in newly laundered shirt and sports jacket. His shoes are polished clean. He has used a touch of Brylcreem on his hair. Brylcreem is all the rage. After all the 'Boys in Blue' advertised it during the Second World War, and Dad is ex-RAF.

We have decorated our father's lorry with coloured paper streamers, put chip baskets end up and lined the 'seats' with packing paper. Our cousins arrive and, with much excitement, we all climb into the back of the lorry. Our father has put up the tarpaulins and slams the tailgate shut. We're off!

On the way, we wave and call out to our friends and relatives as they make their way to the Show. Some are cycling, some walking. Families push their prams. Just a few have cars. There are still horses and carriages. Our own has not long been sold. Our coloured streamers flow gaily in the breeze. Some boys try to cycle fast and catch the paper strands. We laugh and tell them off.

Great-aunt Elise has been collected, by car, and taken to the show by uncle Jack and his wife. Great-aunt Elise has put on her best straw hat, with pearl hat pin. Her long, silk dress was bought at Delas, especially for such occasions.

As we reach the field, to park our lorry, I smell newly-mown grass. I can never smell this scent, now, without thinking of the North Show and Saumarez Park. The lorry bumps over the cut turf and an attendant signals where we must stop. We can see the tent tops in Saumarez Park and hear the brass band. People are streaming in to the gate to buy tickets and get a programme.

We hold hands with the little ones. We are in! There is a merry-go-round and wooden swinging-boats. Loud music, tunes we've heard on the wireless, compete with the band. You can try your luck on the sideshows: hoopla, the coconut shy – or knock down all the piled up tins. My father buys us candy-floss, magically whipped up into sticky pink clouds as you watch. Some of my aunts and uncles play the Crown and Anchor. They often win.

Now, into the main arena and the band music gets louder. Men in red and black uniform march smartly up and down, sliding trombones and beating drums. A man with an echoing loudspeaker tells us what's going on. We manage to get seats and are given voting slips. We watch the fancy-dress competitions and small exhibits, made out of fresh flowers. The scent of flowers mixes with the cut-grass, hot-dogs and chips being cooked somewhere.

In the background we can see the main floats, waiting their turn: a windmill, made of pink and blue hydrangeas and red dahlias; a lorry decorated with bunting and real blooms all around it with a banner saying 'CARNIVAL'.

We in the North are used to midnight raids on our gardens. You woke up in the morning to find all your flower heads missing. Especially hydrangea, dahlia and marigolds. We didn't mind. We knew it was for the Show. Great Uncle Alfred said it saved him from dead-heading anyway.

The large floats start to move around the arena. Pretty girls in party dresses sit on the floats and throw flowers at us. I catch a scarlet rose and blush the same colour. You can leave your seats to inspect the tents. Great-aunt Elise stays where she is. Because of all the pollen she sneezes, loudly. "Oh! I didn't have time to get out my handkerchief!" she apologizes to the people around her. Later, she whispers to me, "I forgot my handkerchief. But I didn't want anyone to think I was bad mannered."

Inside the stuffy, cackling tents we talk to caged budgies, exotic, brightly coloured birds and yellow canaries. We look at the shiny red hens, quacking ducks and proud white geese, all smelling of warm feathers.

Dark eyed rabbits sit quietly, hearts thumping, waiting to be taken home. We compare the guinea pigs with our own and decide ours are just as good. But, no, look at that one! It's as big as a rabbit and has won First Prize.

Great Aunt Elise, Bruce and relations

On to the marvellous displays of truly magnificent home-grown blooms. And there are plates of butter-coloured parsnips, carrots with green tops still on and huge onions with skins like brown paper. Great Uncle Alfred has won a prize for his cabbages. I am pleased. It made up for having to look at our front garden full of cabbages, both side of the path, for weeks on end. I used to half-close my eyes and pretend they were an elegant swathe of green lawn, instead.

A cousin has won third prize for her fruit preserves, but a first for her Victoria sponge. All around us is the bounty of Guernsey's gentle sun: four perfect red tomatoes; four purple plums, blackberries, figs and sloe gin. There are flawless duck eggs and hen's eggs, their shells alabaster white through to dark brown, some still with downy feathers on them.

We think one day we will enter a miniature garden, but never do. We admire the winners. There is a farmyard with matchstick gates and one with a glass pond, the tiny flowerheads look like bushes. Green moss is used for grass and small pebbles for rocks.

Out now, into the bright, fresh air and a search for the tea-tent. But we decide that the queue is too long. We pass the beer tent, smelling of windfall apples in an orchard. Much laughter pours out – getting louder as the day lengthens into evening.

On the day before, always a Wednesday, the cattle were judged, horses and 'fur and feather' put through their paces. Some people only ever went to the Wednesday North Show, claiming it was the *real show*. Farmers and growers alike would meet and talk, comparing their year, sizing up the livestock and making their own judgements on the fine produce on display.

But for us, it was time for the Battle of Flowers. All at once the loudspeaker man yells, "LET BATTLE COMMENCE!" We have been waiting for this! Immediately, we run to the centre of the park where all the judged floats, large and small, have now been placed. We begin to tear out all the flowers – throwing them at each other. The word 'battle' is not for nothing as a large, stinging, hydrangea (stalk and all) whips past my ear. We don't give up until the arena grass is covered with pelted flower heads and we have all got green stains on our clothes and bits of petals and leaves in our hair. Young men climb over the 'Windmill', leaving it picked clean and now just a chicken-wire frame. They gleefully pelt each other, triumphantly destroying this year's *Prix d'Honneur*.

Another show is over. The light is fading as we make our way to the lorry. It is still warm as the evening stars begin to show. The music still plays. Courting couples stroll by and the young people won't leave for some time yet. But we have babies to put to bed.

So, now it is nearly Autumn. Once the North Show has been held, we say, the summer is over. But our island's sun is still warm on our arms. The air softens and the light lowers as in late afternoon. Like the berries, sloes and pears that have been gathered and conserved, we ripen and allow ourselves to slip toward Winter.

Our store of warmth – bathing in our fresh-salt sea, memories of succulent, delicious meals shared outdoors with friends, are safe within us. We face the cold, rainy sea and fields. And let, at last, the thought of Christmas enter our hearts. We are ready, now.

September 11th, 2001, will never be forgotten. Just as, after the Second World War, we children were warned to look out for mines in the sand. We never ran carelessly across the bays of Chouet or L'Ancresse. Our parents spoke ominously of H-bombs and A-bombs. They worried so. But we all came through safely.

And Christmas, the Winter Solstice, heralds the return of the sun. The first, dark green shoot of daffodils are already there well before Boxing Day. And next year will be quite different. But our seasons remain the same and we will never forget.

15 Aunty Frances and Uncle Jack

August 2005

And so the schools have at last broken up and the summer is here. We have had the prize-givings and the sports days. The sports days I remember most were those at the Vale School.

We wore white shirts and navy shorts and a sash across our chests in the colour of our house. Mine was yellow, for Buckingham, red was for Balmoral, blue for Sandringham and green for Windsor.

I was in the yellow house, Cavell, once I got to the Intermediate school as well, but that was because my sister was already there and in Cavell. She was ace at every sport you could mention, captain of most teams and her tie (striped because of all the captaincies) was covered with badges.

The poor unsuspecting teachers put me in Cavell, expecting the same sports performance from me. But I was only good at English and Art and remained permanently in the 'B' teams for swimming and netball. Hockey was beyond me – all that bullying off at the centre made me red-faced, but I enjoyed tennis even though I was just about able to hit the ball back and forth over the net without much grace.

The Vale School sports day was held at Corbet Field. This was most exciting. It had a grandstand, for the Vale Rec football team, and well kept green grass. Even better, my Auntie Frances and Uncle Jack Goubert had built a bungalow right next to Corbet Field so on sports days my mum would take the babies and wave at me from Auntie Frances' garden. After the sports I would toddle off to their bungalow and have some tea.

Next to Auntie Frances was the Goddard's house and they had just begun selling textiles and clothing from their front room. They had a field with a greenhouse in it.

Soon the Goddard's outgrew their home premises and expanded and enlarged their business using the land adjacent. Over a period of years their firm became 'St David's Textiles', then the flourishing 'St David's' that we know now.

Aunty Frances and Uncle Jack –
Frances and Jack Goubert, 1930s

Not far off, in the Capelles, the Mahy family rented out land to campers. They started to sell camping equipment to their customers and they too, expanded. Little by little their business became 'Aladdin's Cave'.

A lot of local families made their living beginning with small ventures. Quite a few started off using greenhouses (what is now the Friquet market garden, the ex-Tomato Museum, The Strawberry Farm, Brouards the Florists and Guernsey Freesia Centre are just a few.)

After the disruptive war, the resourceful, thrifty Guernsey people often turned their hand to bring in much needed cash. There were many needlewomen: Mrs Taylor made her front room into a sewing room and she made my wedding dress and the bridesmaids' dresses from there.

Handmade and homemade clothes were much more common in those days. After much poring over books you would choose your pattern and material from Creaseys and head for your favourite dressmaker. My first dance dress was pink brocade and made by Mrs Underdown.

Door to door selling was much more prevalent and so were 'Club books'. Women selling clothes from Club books made a small commission and some others sold Tupperware at house parties.

Bakers, butchers, greengrocers, milkmen, fishmongers and newsagents all delivered to the door and were paid on Saturdays. There were still the small shops on the corner, often carried out from the wing of a cottage or sheds that had evolved over time to become a business or office. These enterprises were important to our community and I agree with Michelle Laine who recently mourned the passing of Richmond Stores. These places were far more than shops: they were meeting places and focal points for the locals and not replaceable by commercial outlets like garages.

My Uncle Jack made his garage into his office. He was a carpenter and I adored him. He was dark and handsome and drove a smart, modern, black car. I thought he looked like a film star.

When my sports day was over (I usually only ran in the relay race – but once was chosen to do an exhibition on the balancing bars, so perhaps I wasn't a complete athletic duffer), I would hurry over to the red brick bungalow and Uncle Jack. He had made a 'breakfast room' and had a 'study', both of which were practically unheard of in those days.

The average grower didn't have much time or truck for leisurely breakfasts or studies. But not only that, Auntie Frances had a *glass table* in her breakfast room and a coffee percolator! She was the first that I recall to have both a Hoover and a refrigerator. They had a record player as well and a *divan*, for guests.

Even now, when I pass that house I think of Corbet Field and sports day. My own first house, close by, was a semi-detached called The Lee, in L'Islet and it turned out that Uncle Jack had built it. It was a sound little place and close to Grand Havre.

I used to walk my children to the Capelles School, there and back every day. Sometimes, if I drove, I would park at the Guernsey pottery car park (the pottery was just starting out then and you could go in and see people shaping and glazing the pots), then we would drive pass Corbet Field, Route Carré and St David's.

Now, the traffic there is fearsome, whizzing past at a rate of knots, stopping only for the traffic lights. Like everything else, all seems to be rush and hurry.

But I can still remember my yellow sash for Buckingham and taking part in the all important sports of childhood. Anyway: the Vale School yet thrives and so do the far sighted families who worked hard to achieve their dreams. Vision and hard work bring success. At least some things don't change.

16 First Flight

August 2003

Those poor holidaymakers, delayed hours, days even, at Heathrow. And, here we are building a modern new airport, for yet more planes, more travel. Our first airport was tiny, but there was a good tearoom with a mural on the wall. We used to go there for special outings and thought it most exciting and up–to-date. There weren't many flights (with some only via Jersey) and you could drive right up to the door. The *Guernsey Evening Press* published not only the number of flights arriving every day, but a list of the passengers as well.

Yet, I recently met a young woman in her thirties who had never been off the island in her life. We began chatting about Guernsey beanjar, lobsters for supper almost everyday (her son has a boat) and how much simpler and nicer life can be on this island of ours.

My parents never took holidays, either. We didn't once go as a family to foreign holiday resorts, nor to England, either. A two-week break was unheard of. You couldn't leave your livelihood for that length of time.

Our holidays were more like odd days off, here and there, in season. We went to the Muratti in Guernsey and, by excursion boat, to Jersey. Once, as a teenager with friends, we stayed overnight at the Merton Hotel on a special deal. And of course we visited Herm and Sark, always for day trips. Once, in Herm, we tried to bring back a bag of pink shells from shell beach. We had spent all afternoon collecting them, but my great-uncle Alfred made us tip them up on the path before we got on the boat. We howled with anger.

My father-in-law told me how he enjoyed going to Sark when he was younger. He would walk out of his house, in the Forest, without locking it, stay for a night or two in Sark with his pals, and then sail home. There was never any fear of robbery and he did this many times.

The Fermain boat was a treat: after a day on the pebbly beach you'd clamber on to the rocking craft from the wooden pier and chug around the coast to St Peter Port harbour. The dark green trees and banks above the bays looked so pretty, reflected in the sea. We leaned over to trail our hands in the water, as pleased as if we had been away for days.

Edwin Bréhaut, London, 1958

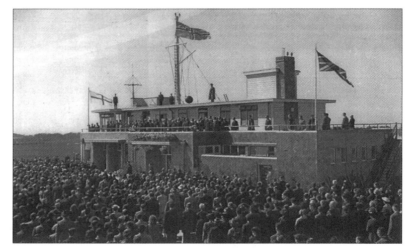

Opening of Guernsey Airport, 1939

Our parents always took us to the North Show, never the South or West – those weren't 'ours'. We would go on the Wednesday, as well, to see the cattle, horses and goats being judged and there would be a gymkhana to watch. The Brocks and the Froomes always won everything, getting all the cups and rosettes. It was hardly worth competing.

In glorious June my great-uncle Alfred liked to hire a chauffered car and we would visit all the prize gardens. He always knew the owners and they discussed gardening completely in patois. My father's preference was the horse races on L'Ancresse Common. He placed bets with the bookies and we knew that the best time to ask for extra pocket money was when he won, which was often.

The annual regattas were favourites, both at St Sampson's and St Peter Port. (Rocquaine regatta was much too far away for us.) Little boats would decorate with flags and lights. There would be competitions, a funfair and music playing late into the night. We thought it was all very glamorous as we danced on the harbour. Dad would buy us chips on the way home.

Floodlit swimming Galas at La Valette were quite an event. You sat on the rocks to watch swimmers and divers compete against Jersey. There was a diving board then and Havelet was a fashionable place. In 1953 my mother and I visited relations in Southend. We went by boat and train (my first remembered train ride, was aged 11). I upset my aunt by saying "Where's the sea?" as I gazed at what looked like a long mudbank, swirling with dirty grey water.

"Well, at least we have a wonderful outdoor pool!" my aunt exclaimed. But the blue-tiled pool smelt of chlorine and was nothing like our seawater pools at Havelet. I longed to go home.

My first flight was with my father when I was 16. I embarrassed him by being terrified. The flight seemed to last for ages and I clung to my seat all the way. We stayed at the Strand Palace Hotel. My father did some business at Covent Garden and I went to the National Art Gallery with my Guernsey-born boyfriend, who was then living in London. We went for a coffee in Chelsea. This was the beginning of the swinging sixties and, even then, there was an air of being in the right place at the right time, in the most trendy place in the world. Even now, I visit the National Art Gallery every year.

Back in beautiful Guernsey, after a day sunbathing on the beach, locals and visitors could see live Cabaret entertainment. All the main hotels put on professional shows. Ronnie Corbet and Little and Large did summer seasons here. Ronnie Corbet was a natural comic and we got to know him. "Come home with me for a sandwich," he joked, cuddling one of our friends, "or perhaps a roll on the carpet!"

So it was, that apart from France, my first 'abroad' holiday was when I was forty years-old. The flight took four hours and was to Greece. Here, in the Mediterranean, I saw people just like my own: swimming daily in the sea, whole families together, promenading then eating fresh food out of doors. Their supper was whatever the fisherman brought to shore. Even the sea was like ours – tourquoise shot through with blue and violet, the sea so clear you could see the sand below.

But, fortunately, we don't have to endure Heathrow, Gatwick and Stansted. Our wonderful island is just on our doorsteps. All we have to do is appreciate what our own gem of the sea has to offer. Not 'guaranteed sun', no. Nor, though, the problems that go with that: drought, mosquitoes, searing heat and failed crops.

We need to stop, stand and stare, sometimes. Seek out the wild and untouched. There are, even now, unexpected places in Guernsey that can take your breath away. For, right here in our little Guernsey, you can still find paradise.

17　The Muratti

February 2005

We went to the Muratti football game every year when we were teenagers. It was one of the highlights of the year, like the North Show, horseracing on L'Ancresse Common and the North Regatta. Sometimes, when the Muratti was held in Jersey we would take the special offer of going over by boat and stay one night at the Merton Hotel. Since there was no television then it was the only way of seeing the match live, but it meant taking two days off from work and the ferry took hours to and from Guernsey and Jersey.

If the match was played in Guernsey, we took a bus to the Half Way and walked down Victoria Avenue to The Track stadium. It was very exciting and we would dress in our best.

The star players around that time were Len Duquemin – 'The Duke,' Bill Spurdle and Les Collins. I wasn't really interested in football, but liked the atmosphere at The Track and it was a chance to parade before the boys.

I don't remember sitting on the chairs around the pitch, although they were provided. It was more fun to walk around, chatting to friends sitting and standing on the grassy banks. Some young men climbed the trees for a good vantage point. Music played through loudspeakers, strung to the branches.

My father was a great football fan and knew all the catchprases that were called out in unison, "Eeesay! Eeesay!" when Jersey was being beaten and "Any*where*! Any*where*!" when the ball was wildly kicked to no-one in particular. It was a lot of enjoyment and everyone joined in good-naturedly. If the green and whites won over the red and whites, well, we were ecstatic. If Jersey won we were bitterly disappointed. After the match we streamed out in our hundreds up Track Lane and queued for the bus home.

Recently my mother Mary Bréhaut, a lifelong supporter of Manchester United (as was my father) and I plus several members of my family had the good fortune to be invited to a Private Box at Old Trafford.

We flew direct to Manchester Airport and booked in to a nearby hotel that seemed to cater solely for Man United fans. Before the match we raided the shop and bought Man United red shirts with 'Vodaphone' on the front and our favourite players' name and number on the back. We even wore them to breakfast in the hotel next day, as did nearly all the fans staying overnight. Yes football includes advertising now and big money – that is the way the 'beautiful game' has gone. All sports now need their backers, as do all of the arts. What used to be natural, uncomplicated and traditional skills have all been affected by global big business. Think of Ellen MacArthur and B & Q!

Yvonne and cousin Adèle Sheppard, 1950s

Amongst our party were members of the Guernsey branch Manchester United Club one of whom had met Sir Matt Busby and seen George Best play. Through the kindness of some local Manchester United directors we were treated to complimentary programmes and a delicious meal with waiter service. It was a real treat.

We saw David Beckham lead Man United to a 2-1 win against Tottenham Hotspur. We were able to relay the roar of the crowd into the box with an optional sound system and the excitement of seeing the match live was something none of us will forget.

In our box we also had a television screen upon which replays were shown. The knowledgeable supporters knew of these screens and placed themselves in front of the private boxes with their soundproof glass windows. Although we couldn't hear what they were saying, they waved their hands and made us understand that we should turn the screen around so that they could see it as well! Of course we complied and we really felt part of the occasion.

After the match, the supporters gave us thumbs up and we waved back. Some of them had come a long way to support their team and there wasn't an empty seat in a stadium taking some 67,000 people.

So, this year our Muratti will be staged like a Premiere League game, all ticketed, all seated. Now held at Foote's Lane and with its new stadium, extra seating and a large screen it certainly won't be the same as our old Murattis at The Track. But then, those were of the Fifties and Sixties.

In 1966 England won the World Cup. Bobby Moore, the team captain, was considered to be a God. Yet, he earned far, far less than the Owens and Rooneys of today. It is 2005 now and football talent attracts sponsors.

Sponsors want a return on their investment – paying customers – and the customers want something different for *their* money. And, we are told, quite a sizeable slice of the sponsor's money will be ploughed back into supporting local football.

It is all a far cry from the simple enjoyable occasion of watching local lads do good on a green pitch down The Track. But in those days everything *was* more simple: we had less money to spend and, arguably, far more sense of community.

So the Muratti is going to cost more, with top tickets reckoned to be at £12. Well, at least we've got plenty of time to save. About a quid a week should do it. I wonder if the footballers themselves might even be encouraged to up their game in such prestigious surroundings?

We've got some excellent players who might well go on to join the Beckhams and the Le Tissiers. And if this year's amateur Muratti is anything even remotely like the professional Old Trafford game we saw, it should be worth every penny.

18 Cabbages

Work has started on our new Market. They have found some wonderful French art nouveau tiling in the former Podger's sports shop, later called Sarnia Sports. Podger's, we learn, used to belong to a fruiterer named Thomas & Mowat.

I remember, when I worked in the shop one summer, aged 16, how cold it used to be. All around were the open stalls of fruit, vegetables and flowers and the wind and rain whipped into the entrances. Further on were the butchers and the fishermen's stalls, serving their regular customers, day after day. Whatever the weather, Podger's doors stayed open, with goods displayed on the pavcmcnt outside. But we had ways of combating the cold.

I recall being sent off to the family-run cafe above Market Steps. The aroma of freshly ground coffee drifted over the cool morning air guiding me there. I trotted back to the shop with a tray of hot, milky coffee in a jug and homemade cakes toped with coffee butter cream. We soon warmed up.

On Wednesdays, a bus trip home for lunch was made more cheerful by the thought of a rich casserole with pork and haricot beans, just like the Norman cassoulet. There would be Guernsey biscuits and squares of apple or rhubarb pie, made *enter daeux craoutes* – between two crusts. I returned to work much comforted.

Sometimes my young brother would come to Town, wanting me to take him to Le Cheminant's toy shop in the Arcade. Or, we might have to go down to Baker's Bazaar in the Pollet and stand behind the rail, pointing out what he wanted to the shop assistant. Now and then I'd take him to Maison Carré's coffee shop – upstairs – above what is now known as Dix-Neuf. There, we could watch the shoppers, bags in hand and meeting friends for a chat.

In my great-aunt Elise and grandmother's kitchen there were always pots on top of the oven and covered dishes simmering inside it. Even now I remember the smell of belly pork, onions and haricot beans and also oxtail, cooked slowly all night so that when you ate it, the rich meat fell apart in its beefy juices. We'd eat it with potatoes roasted in beef dripping. In the same oven, sultana rock cakes and scones were baked for Thursday's *visite*.

On Sundays a rice pudding, cooked in its earthenware pot, got its name from *houichepotte* (the last hayload in the field). Normandy has the same dish, a *tergoule*, cooked in a special, glazed terrine to serve up after a long day outdoors.

With plentiful supplies of home-grown vegetables, soups were always on the go and a stockpot always kept. My grandmother made brawn, suet plum puddings and rich conger soup, poached in milk. She cooked for my grandfather while he tended his tomato crop, the pigs, chickens and ducks. Grandmother Bréhaut loved eating crispy bacon rinds and suet puddings. Her sole advice to young couples for a long marriage was, "You should stick it out, like we had to."

Mondays and Tuesdays were laundry days, so leftovers were made into cottage pies and pasties. On a cold winter's day, soaking wet from my bike ride down the big hill from the Vale school, I'd smell cabbage or lentil soup. They were delicious, eaten with a warm pasty. The bike ride back to school was harder going, all uphill, but my cheeks were rosy red.

After the war, my father-in-law would never eat carrots. He'd had hardly anything else to eat during the Occupation. Even the sight of them turned him off. My father threw cans of Spam out of the house. He, too, had had more than enough of it when he served in the RAF, in India and Burma.

My father-in-law liked lettuce cut into strips and sprinkled with sugar. Lettuce was only eaten in season, save for Boxing Day when my mother in-law bought a hot-house one at what she thought was gross expense. She saved the top of full-cream Guernsey milk (the only sort available then) each day in a Kilner jar. Then, on Friday evenings, she would add salt to the saved milk and hand-churn a butter pat, ready for Saturday. It was kept wrapped in cabbage leaves and placed in the pantry.

Hand-pressed tongue and thick, home-cured ham was for Boxing Day. They were a great delicacy in the late Forties. Rationing was just ending and 'luxury' food carefully used. We had capon, chicken, goose or beef for Christmas Day, never turkey.

Turkey was an American idea that hadn't yet reached us. And there was no Coca-Cola or McDonalds. Our culture was still our own. Long before organic food became fashionable, Guernsey people grew runner

Original tiles found in Podger's Sports Shop

The tea shop, St Peter Port, 1958

beans, peas, potatoes and onions. Knowing how to grow, preserve and keep food before households had fridges or freezers was a necessity.

In amongst the flowers in spring grew chives and radishes. Each patch of rich earth had its twigged arch for the scarlet runners. *Vraic* was still used as a rich and free fertiliser. It still can.be used at certain times in the year. I remember whole fields at Chouet covered with seaweed, smelling of pungent sea-salt, lending the soil its iodine goodness.

In June and July mackerel were plentiful and ormers were fried, stewed and pickled. Our seashore bounty yielded chancres, lobsters and lady crabs – all eaten plain with vinegar and bread and butter. But now, our wonderful Markets have gone. People buy their sandwiches, made in England and chilled in freezers.

Takeaway and prepared food is everywhere. It is from all parts of the world. All is rush and race.

Still, there are still shops like the one in the Forest that sells things from Guernsey, Alderney, Sark and France. Sometimes you can get oysters from Herm. Our hedgerows burgeon with lovely home-grown produce, sold on trust.

Our ancestors worked hard and ate well. My great-aunt Elise die aged 80, great-uncle Alfred at 96, my father at 90 and my grandmother at 100. You are what you eat? *Pour saeure!*

19 Phone a Friend

February 2004

"What's the fastest way of spreading news? Telegraph, telephone, tell a woman!" (One of my fathers' favourite jokes). Everywhere, now, people are telling everyone, it seems, something every second of every day. Mobiles in cars, in hospitals, shops, and streets – news even if you don't want it.

My great-aunt Elise had a telephone in her hall. It was shiny black, fixed to the wall and had a dial with large numbers. This was her entertainment. She would stand and chat to her friends as often as she could. I'd hear,

"Coumciq l afaire va?" (how are things going?),

"J'sis vrai!" (I'm right!),

"Nen-nin dja!" (No, indeed),

"J n sae pui" (I don't know at all),

"I me-t avis ke," (it seems to me that), long before I knew what the patois actually meant.

Before dialing came (in Guernsey in 1955) calls were made through a telephonist. You would wind the handle at the side to connect to the telephonist (nearly always a woman) and tell her what number you wanted. There were several telephone exchanges in parishes such as St Peter's, and the main one in Town, opposite Elizabeth College.

Sometimes you got cut off. With my first job in an office, at Huelin's on North Side, St Sampson's, I had to do relief telephone duty. You wore heavy headphones complete with mouthpiece. The rack of white balls in front of you all had an extension number. When calls came through, you shoved in a lead to connect the caller, then transfer the call to whoever they wanted to talk to. I regularly cut people off and would frantically ring Paddy down in the coal order department to help me. He always did, and always knew what to do.

Huelins also had, then, an up-to-date Gestetner copying machine. A monster which needed to be fed thick black ink. You typed your words on a special flimsy sheet, fitted it to the machine and rolled a handle, like a mangle. This way many copies could be made of the document.

The first time I used it I was wearing a white pleated skirt. It never did recover from the mess I made.

After that were telex, another horrendous system of coded hole-punching on a roll of paper which made the later fax machines a doddle. Now there is e-mail, a wonderful way of sending messages – and no telephone skills needed. Excellent.

I had a friend who was a telephonist. She was a very good knitter, as well. When she phoned you she would keep breaking off to put someone through and then continue knitting and talking to me through her headphones. She knitted some lovely jumpers and cardigans whilst at work. Helping people to make their telephone calls was fitted in – more as an incovenience if anything. Her calls to me took ages and I would eye the pile of dishes to be done and the meal to be cooked as she happily nattered away, her needles clicking, another ball of wool unraveling.

Telephones used mainly to be fixed to the wall. People rarely had more than one and they were always black. Usually they would be in the hall with a chair close by. It was considered to be very grand to have an extension (unheard of for children to have their own line) and very upmarket to have a coloured one, say white or red.

And calls were always answered (no Ansaphones). The ringing bell was very loud, not easily ignored. In our first home we had a party line. This meant that sometimes you picked up the receiver and the other sharers were in mid-speech. We would tell each other to get off the line, thank you, and try later. First come, first served.

A trunk call, to Australia or America (for instance), could be booked beforehand and left a pause between what you said and what the other person said. So that you ended up talking to an echo. And it was very expensive.

Today's mobile telephones can send messages by text, take photographs, send those photographs to your computer, play games and all but make a cup of tea. They are no longer *just* for making conversations but are cameras, notepads, entertainment and monitoring aids. "Where are you? What time are you coming home?" And, in the shops, "Do you fancy beef or lamb tonight? I'm in Safeways..." I hear personal details of people's lives I would much rather not.

Telephone voices are quite different from their normal easy-going rhythm. We have become used to the interruption in our daily lives of a kind of human lift music – a babble, unwanted and subliminal.

Taking a telephone call used to be very personal and formal. You never phoned if you thought someone might be having a meal, or busy with a visitor. But now, if you own a mobile you can be contacted at all times. No longer the seat in the hall, too bad if you are on the beach or in the park. You must speak and you must speak now. Not only that,

Yvonne and Bruce Bréhaut, 1958

Guernsey Telephone Exchange, 1950s

78

now they can have a picture of where you are as well, and send one of them to you, which can be sent to their computer and fixed for all time. So much for privacy.

On holiday in France we mobile-phoned our friends in Italy. They were in the swimming pool, we were in a restaurant. "How's the weather with you?" There was no urgency, we just wanted to chat. Madness, isn't it? What happened to postcards? Still, much better than trying to find a public telephone box and finding it needed a card, or was vandalized.

How history would be re-written if mobile telephones had been available to the soldiers of world wars one and two. Imagine telephoning from the trenches. "We're just about to go over the top, mum..!" "I can see the landing beaches of Normandy." How horrifically real those wars would have been. How immediate Iraq was. How involved we became.

On the fateful aeroplanes that crashed on September 11th in the New York offices, people sent final mobile and text messages of love to devastated friends and relations. A sad and terrible use that could not have been imagined.

I have a mobile and use it if I remember to charge it, but mostly switch it off. I never did get on with telephones. Must be something to do with all those rolling white eyeballs at Huelins. Paddy's not around to help me, either.

Oh, it's all too much for words!

20 Dancing Days

November 2005

It was a sunny day in September 1959 and I sat on the sandbank at the top of Ladies Bay and ate an ice-cream. I had worked at Podger's Sports Shop all that summer and they had franchised the Kiosk at Ladies Bay where I sometimes helped out, but it was my day off.

Along the path of the common headland, coming from Chouet, I saw my cousin with his best friend. The best friend was riding along slowly on a brand new 500cc motor bike. Motor bikes were all the rage in those days – the more powerful the better.

As they drew up alongside me the best friend asked if I would like to hop on the back for a spin. I thought he meant that he would just turn in a circle, just to show the bike off. But he suddenly sped onto the road going from the Amarreurs and then turned left to L'Ancresse. Suddenly we were on a main road. I hung on for dear life as the boy revved the engine and we tore along at about 90 miles an hour. I was wearing a light top, trousers, flip-flops and no crash helmet. He wasn't wearing one either.

As we zipped past the slipway at L'Ancresse and turned the slight bend toward Pembroke tearooms, it happened. A hire car, coming in the opposite direction, driven by a Frenchman, turned in front of us. His bumper caught my leg and I was thrown off.

I lay on the sandy turf feeling very foolish. I saw the motorbike and rider disappear past the tearooms. I was alone. I made to stand up but found that I couldn't. I looked around me. Several people were beginning to form a crowd, encircling me. Again, I tried to rise but was unable to.

The people began to look aghast. Then I looked down and saw the horrible truth. The aluminium bumper had torn back the skin on my leg and there was a deep gash on my ankle from which was pouring a fountain of blood. I grasped my ankle, trying to stem the flow, only to realise that I could see the white bone beneath. Then I screamed.

Someone rushed over to me with a towel, in order to check the streaming blood. I could see sand and grass inside the wound. I thought I would get lockjaw, like we had always been warned about. I wanted my mum.

*Yvonne, aged 17,
Channel Islands Hotel*

An ambulance arrived and I was taken to the Princess Elizabeth Hospital. I remember seeing my mother's face and telling her not to worry. The operation took six hours. My main tendons had been severed. I was seventeen.

I woke up next morning with a kind of tent over my legs. Convinced that I had lost my foot I peeked under the sheets. There was my foot, and I was plastered in white up to my knee. But, left unplastered, I could see all five toes. I wondered if they were somehow put there – maybe artificial ones in plastic? – to ease any shock. So I wiggled them and found, thankfully, that they were indeed my own toes.

There was a matron at the PEH in those days and GPs used to come and visit you on their rounds. Dr Kellett-Smith was pleased with my steady progress although I was furious to have missed a very hot Indian summer.

The recovery took a good year and my ankle is still scarred and weak. But Dr Kellett-Smith had made a marvellous job of stitching the tendons together so that I could walk again. For physiotherapy I had to go to Mr Kennard, in his lovely town house almost opposite the Queen's Road surgery. Treatment included dipping my ankle several times in a bath of hot wax before Mr Kennard kneaded the damaged area so that the tendons and other tissues wouldn't stick together. I found this excruciating.

I used to go to Mr Kennard on the bus – one from our house in Route Militaire then another one up the Grange. A chap who had damaged his knee used to have the same routine. We had been at school together and his girlfriend worked at the States Insurance office situated by the then Police Station and opposite the Old Government House Hotel. We would hobble down the Grange and then into Town where he could see

81

his girlfriend for a little chat.

Mr Kennard said that dancing would be a very good form of exercise. So I began going with a gang of both male and female cousins to the Channel Islands Hotel. The boys would take turns to help me slowly dance around the floor.

By coincidence my husband-to-be saw me on the night that the photograph was taken and wanted to ask me to dance, until he saw the crutches. But we did meet up a few months later at St George's Hall.

Gradually I learnt to walk without a limp. Although negotiating Petit Bot pebbles was and still is quite difficult. I find cobbles hard going as well so always walk up the Town High Street using the flatter gutter. I have been walking in the gutter for some 46 years now.

Medicine was much simpler in those days. There wasn't a lot of choice, far more given by injection and you didn't make a fuss. Just this week I was given some antibiotics. I read the enclosed information:

Possible side effects: can cause stomach problems, vomiting, diarrhoea and pins and needles; jaundice and other liver disorders which can be fatal in rare circumstances; allergies, difficulty in breathing and swelling which may need emergency treatment. Ulceration of the mouth and sloughing off of the skin. Rarely, teeth can become discoloured which can be cured by professional cleaning. There have been reports of dizziness, difficulty sleeping, hallucinations, changes in heart rhythm, inflammation of the pancreas and convulsions.

If you develop any of these problems consult your doctor.

Are they *kidding*? Bring back matron, is what I say and a society where everyone is not suing everyone else at the merest hint of things going wrong.

I didn't get any compensation for the damage to my leg. The French man went back to France. My cousin's friend still sped on his motorbike until old PC Trotter got him. But at least I threw away my crutches and I have been dancing ever since.

21 Christmas Spirit

December 2005

Oh dear. This year I have done most of my shopping by the Internet. It is so easy: Amazon tell me by e-mail when they have the top ten books sometimes at half-price or at least heavily discounted. I enter my password (they already have my credit card details) and the books arrive a couple of days later, with no VAT added. This procedure can be followed with many other companies and I can buy anything – clothes, shoes, toys even food and drink via the Internet.

But shoppers like me have led to the demise of Grut's. Randalls are going and Creasey's are worried. Dearie me. What ever is to be done? Time was when Christmas shopping was the only time that people went to Town. Carefully hoarded savings would be drawn in cash – or chequebooks would be full in time for the extra shopping. Credit cards didn't exist nor even computers, let alone the Internet.

A time-honoured routine was followed – meat and poultry ordered weeks ahead and fresh parsley, thyme and freshly grown lettuce eagerly pounced on no later than a day before Christmas Eve. Christmas trees would be collected (needles dropping all over the place) and the decorations would be years old, kept in a box in the attic.

But what fun it all was! And that, I believe, will be the saving of local shops. Christmas shopping, mingling with the crowds in Town and the Bridge, and the out of town scattered villages like Cobo, St Martin's and St Peter's is fun. We are all bent on the same mission – to have a lovely family time with all the festive trimmings. And why not?

Outside it is cold and dark. The solstice, happening just before Christmas Eve – the return of the sun, won't make a great deal of difference for some weeks yet. So we show some light and warmth in our homes just for a few days. We prepare and plan and forget about the sleet and driving rain as we dream of the delicious food awaiting us and the roaring log fires.

And it is good to meet friends in our High Street and maybe have a drink with them or a meal afterwards. In restaurants, cafés and pubs, laden with parcels, any chill is forgotten as we huddle up in groups and stave off the worst elements of winter.

The Christmas lights sparkle in the gloom and shops have gone the extra mile with decorated Christmas trees, Santa's grottos and December flowers. Yes, the cash tills ring, but what the heck? It's only for once a year. Over the years we always went to Grut's for the special presents, for good leather luggage and special party clothes for children. They kept a good selection of Christmas cards: for our 'specials': Mother, Father, Son, Daughter, Grandma and Grandpa. Cards you don't want from a selection box.

Yvonne and Bruce Bréhaut, 1947

You'd get to know the ladies and gents behind the counter of Grut's, Creasey's and the now lost Keyho's. Already gone are Delas, Cokers and Du Bras. Whoever would have thought that Brennans would close down or Leale's come to that?

Shopping in the old days meant that you changed into your best outdoor clothes, with a good winter coat, gloves and scarves. Some made their winter coat last years, only the fashion conscious would buy a coat every year, and almost always you only had one coat, one raincoat maybe and a jacket – not several of each. Why would you want more? You replaced what wore out.

Once ready, a housewife would board a bus, complete with her shopping basket, bag and purse. If it was windy she might wear a headscarf – and would probably receive at least one new one at Christmas. She would wear sensible shoes for walking around the market, and be on conversational terms with her butcher and fishmonger. He would know exactly what she wanted, which cut and at what price. He would address her as 'Mrs' or 'Miss' and realise that bad service or bad products would lose her custom. Her butcher would save marrow bones for her, for her beanjar, and let her know what he was getting in for next week. Thankfully there are still places like this in Guernsey and you will know who they are. No Internet, then, for you, I'm sure.

So, ultimately, there is hope for local shops. Because it really isn't very festive sitting in front of a computer screen on your own, ordering things from a machine, however nice they are and of good value. I will be going into Town, and visiting my favourite local butchers and grocery store because Christmas is the one time when people come first. Being with family and friends, attending Carol Services and the annual Pantomime are important to us.

Christmas allows us to do that. To thank people and to show our love and appreciation. Multiply that love by millions, all over the world and we get the perfect Christmas spirit.

No amount of technical wizardry will fulfil the human satisfaction of giving and receiving in person. The Internet has its place in commerce, but so does the local store. Guernsey people might have lost many of their landmarks but shopping has the same value as going to the cinema instead of watching a video on your own: "It's the experience that counts".

The excitement, the buzz, the celebration of Christmas is once more upon us. I wish everyone a happy time and peaceful New Year.

22 In like a Lion

March has always seemed such a brave little month, to me. It sees the back of Winter, while showing us the hope of Spring. As a child I used to think of it 'marching' over the land, like an army soldier: one minute the earth is warm and full of yellow daffodils and shiny celandines; the next, snow flurries harden the ground and ice clings underneath shady banks.

In my family, March has seen winter sadness, the death of my father, March 2nd, Spring happiness with memories of my parents' wedding anniversary on March 22nd and the birth of their fifth and last child, Elizabeth, March 3rd, fifty years ago this year.

I was twelve and my mother had just come home from the maternity hospital. She gave me my new baby sister to hold. From the shawl gazed a perfect little face. A real beauty. "Now, take care of her, and your mother," said my Aunt, sternly. She had brought my mother home. "You must help her and look after her."

After rushing home from school and the excitement of waiting to see the new addition, I felt a bit daunted. I never did like housework. But that disappointment soon faded as family life moved on.

In the Fifties there was a television programme, called 'Tonight'. Cliff Michelmore was the anchorman and the superb reporters included such icons as Derek Hart, Alan Wicker and (my heartthrob in those days,) Kenneth Alsop. Fyfe Robertson was the witty cameraman and 'Tonight', in black and white, had a catchy signature tune, which Elizabeth used to sing to as a small child. She also loved 'Davy Crockett', then a serial. She would sing: "Davee, Davee Cwocket, kink (king) of the why (wild) fwonteeer"! We thought her words were much better than the real thing. She loved to watch my elder sister and I get ready to go out on a Saturday night. 'Juke Box Jury' would be on TV and we would dance about to the latest pop song.

And Elizabeth had imaginary pigs which she kept at the top of Solidor's garden. Sweet enough, but Great Uncle Alfred actually used to give her food for them – cabbages and left-over peelings. Elizabeth would take strangers to see her pigs and if they didn't know what she meant, well, we didn't let on.

We loved the beaches near us, fishing at the Dolly Rock and endless summer days, swimming off the big pier. Nearly all our friends came from families of four or five children. Couples, parted for so long during the war, often started a 'second' family when they were reunited. (Most of them had come back, stayed together and got on with their lives, with typical Guernsey determination.)

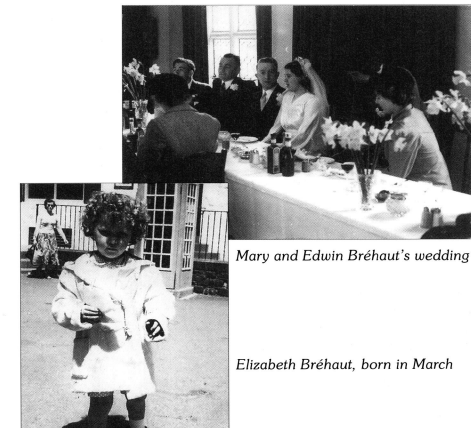

Mary and Edwin Bréhaut's wedding

Elizabeth Bréhaut, born in March

So les Amarreurs, Chouet and the bays near us were playgrounds. Older children often had two or three brothers and sisters with them. We wandered over the rocks and pools: little gangs knowing every inch of our territory. As the March winds blew, on our walks across the common, sand flying in our *eyes*, I longed for the sunny days to come. And March is such a mixture of Alice in Wonderland's mad March hare. Of John Masefield's:

> Dirty British coaster, with a salt-caked smoke stack,
> Butting through the Channel in the mad March days...

Which made me think of 'our' English Channel, and of my father going to the White Rock with his lorry and a load of tomatoes for the UK markets. Of gales, rain and yet burgeoning blossoms, buds and delicate green leaves, tipping the winter-bare branches.

March, (Mars in French), of the war god, also has the threatening ides on March 15th ('Beware the ides of March'). Yet, on the other hand holds the happy celebrations of Mothering Sunday, March 21st and the European holiday, a real Holy Day – the Annunciation – when the angel Gabriel told Mary she had been chosen by God to bear his only son, is celebrated on March 25th.

At Easter, when baby Elizabeth was christened, my mother bought a yellow costume. And she wore a yellow straw hat with a veil sprinkled with lemon coloured dots. Now Easter always means the yellow of Spring, to me. And I can still see that straw hat and still think of chocolate Easter eggs, when I do.

Lent has already begun and Easter is not so far away. March, as it closes, brings us out of the cold as we change our clocks forward. We can begin to think, at least, of warmer days, Jersey Royals and peas from the vegetable garden. And mackerel!

The birds are beginning to nest. The light-green dawn comes sooner – minute by minute the days lengthen. The Winter solstice, on December 21st, seems a long time ago. The Vernal equinox (when day and night are equal) falls on March 21st. That's March. When day and night are equal. When light and dark, cold and warmth, when peace and war struggle with each other to gain a foothold. But at last, all in good time, March's lamb will be born and the roar of the hurtling, ice-cold winds will fade.

Another Winter, another Spring. We have survived, thus far.

Happy Birthday, Elizabeth.

23 Last Little Haven

January 2002

St Sampson's Harbour and its shops are the Guernsey people's own. We always just called it 'The Bridge'. Here, as we shopped, we met lifelong friends, cousins and mates. This is where generations of growers, fishermen, builders and boat-builders shared their daily lives.

You didn't dress up to go to the Bridge. Not as you would if you were going to Town. You could buy a paper at Tozer's, chat to your friends as you picked up fresh bread, then on to Johns the Butcher. You always met someone you knew at the South Side café.

If Guernsey's head is in St Peter Port, her spirit in the middle and upper parishes, then her heart is surely in the Vale and St Sampson's. The Bridge belongs to the Guernsey northerner. This is where the sky is lighter, the air warmer. It is less windy than the south. There is a quiet assurance of centuries gone by. If you live in the Vale and St Sampson's you see the ugly chimneys, the gas tanks and saturation housing every day – so often that you don't even notice them any more.

Huelin's offices have gone – and Leale's. The coal lorries no longer ply up and down, taking coal from Bird's and W A Nicholls to the vineries. But there is still the North Social, the Mariners Inn and the Trafalgar Arms. The North Regatta is alive and well.

Once, when I was young, a woman said to me, haughtily, "You live in the industrial end of the island, don't you?" I didn't know what she meant.

The loose stone walls, home to myriad wild flowers and the quiet lanes where we walked held no threat of dark satanic mills to us! We loved walking through the lanes, laced through with sunny light and wondered what 'industrial' meant. Little gardens were bordered with golden gorse and broom. Spiky palm trees and tamarisk grew in abundance. Off the beaten track, cottages were built, close to the beach, with fishing boats upturned in the back yard for winter. Through the open fields we found familiar boundaries.

Lie in a northern meadow and listen to the evening blackbird's song echoing in the cooling air. In the wide blue sky see the sparrowhawk hover, almost still as it eyes its prey. White clouds, edged in grey and

North Regatta: Mary, Bruce, Yvonne, Maureen and baby Margaret Bréhaut

St Sampson's Bridge, 1911

pink, drift slowly by. As we walk, we see people working their small-holdings. They used to save up to marry and buy a plot.

Not so very long ago, a couple would build a bungalow and make a good living from growing tomatoes and flowers. The wife would help and the children, too, when they came home from school. Long before it was smart to own a yacht, the Guernseyman had a fishing boat. Often you would go out for the day, pottering off Bordeaux. Sometimes we'd take a picnic – crab sandwiches and a flask of tea – and fish off Herm and Sark. There's nothing like your own lobster and mackerel for supper. These fishermen were neither farmers nor townies. We lived in the flat, sandy part of Guernsey. And, once cut off from the main island, Braye du Valle, L'Islet, the Saltpans, the Bridge, we knew the meaning of all these places.

In the Vale and St Sampson's the first Guernseymen settled. L'Ancresse Common holds secrets of many thousands of years – older yet than the Pyramids. St Sampson's Church is the oldest on the island. All the northern bays and coves, from the Vaugrat to Bordeaux, the Bridge and St Sampson's harbour, are sisters. Each is linked and inseparable.

We like to think we were the most like Normandy, the most French. My great-uncles and aunts, grandparents and parents all spoke the northern patois. You can still hear it down the Bridge. Sometimes I fancy I can still see them: bags in hand, bikes parked on the shop wall, chattering away.

People used to say: "I'm from the Vale, me!" with pride. And they still do.

The harbour has seen excellent ship-building, sending fine Guernsey vessels to faraway seas, long, long ago. It has been a safe haven for every craft, big or small, and of every cost. Tankers still come to Guernsey, to St Sampson's Harbour, bringing essentials for all of our islanders.

But the Bridge has more than charm, more than history. Through its workaday, weekday bustle, stop on the busy pavement. You'll hear something quite extraordinary: this little place has a heartbeat.

It is said that St Sampson's Harbour must be changed. There must be more mooring. There should be a new marina. But the Guernsey boat owners more than anyone else will know if this is true or not.

So, perhaps the old girl needs a clean-up. But a clean up, not a facelift. This harbour is a living place. A scalpel cut might leave her different, more modern. But will she ever look the same? Will we recognise our dear old friend? If change does come, remember this is where Guernsey people can be and have been themselves since time began. Many of us make a living now in the Town. Many own leisure boats, that is the way things have gone.

And yet this is still the home of the toilers of the sea – and always will be.

This is, indeed, their last little haven.

24 The Guernsey Press

March 2003

In 1958 I was seventeen and had just started a new job at the Guernsey Press. I was a typist in the offices above the shop in Smith Street. In those days if you didn't have shorthand you couldn't be called a secretary. But 'The Press' didn't need my shorthand, so I was a 'typist'. But I didn't care about that because I loved my job.

Mr Emile and Mr Alf Digard were my bosses and Mr Gervais Peek the Chairman. These three gentlemen were part of a dynasty which still produces our newspaper today. At eleven o'clock each day, on the dot, the three of them would disappear for a 'liquid lunch' at the Coal Hole, the pub at the bottom of the Prince of Wales. In an office of three other girls one of us would then quickly nip over to the cake shop opposite (now a chemist), to buy warm jam doughnuts and we'd have a read of the early edition of the *Star*.

Mr Machon was the editor of the *Star* and Mr Roussel the editor of the *Guernsey Press*. They had separate offices but shared reporters and us office staff. At that time such legendaries as Dave Prigent, Rex Bennett, Herbie Winterflood, Cyd Gardener, Victor Coysh and Carel Toms were employed by the *Press*. The printing presses were at the back of the building and there was a proof-reader, art and photography departments. Next to our office was Mr Paul Le Moal and his assistant. He ran the printing shop.

I had wanted to go to art college or read English at university after Grammar School, but it wasn't possible. So, sometimes I'd hang around the artists, watching them produce work on advertising and so on, wondering if I would ever get anything printed in the *Press* myself.

My typewriter was manual and you needed to put carbon paper between every sheet if you wanted more copies. There was no photocopier and no computers. My desk faced the door. One day it was decided that I should have a 'vanity panel' fixed in front of my desk, to hide my legs. At the time the *Press* were having a campaign against the destruction of places of natural interest. Imagine my surprise when a group of reporters arrived in our office, waving placards which read 'Down with the Vanity Panel', 'Save our place of natural interest'. Mr Emile and the girls started laughing. But I had to

Yvonne, going to work, 1959

have the joke explained!

The accounts were done by adding machine and a huge Comptometer, which took up much space. Comptometer operators were highly valued and high on the pecking order. This was because the machine was a complicated monster with a mind of its own.

In the print room the men would carefully place individual blocks of lead texts to be inked and printed on the newspaper. Everything was black and white and the workshop was always very busy and noisy.

In the *Press* shop, managed by Mr Maindonal, people could take their family messages for the *Press*. Hatches, matches and despatches we called them. It was fun to always know the news first and since the business was all about words and pictures I never liked a job more.

We would take the bus to work into town every morning. Single people rarely had cars. They might get a lift in, but mostly we all travelled by bus. I liked to look at the sea as we trundled in to St Peter Port. Every day it was different, sometimes choppy and grey, other times smooth and sparkling. Always, on the horizon, there were the little islands, with the sun on them, or cold and distant if it was raining and misty.

Once in to town, I'd rush up High Street, into work, making coffee for the others the first task, since I was the junior. For lunch, bought sandwiches were unheard of. If you had sandwiches you made them yourself, with a cake made by Mum, perhaps, and an apple. We'd take ours down to the harbour on sunny days and hitch up our skirts to get our legs brown. And I liked to window shop at Bon Marche, Smith Street. I could only afford, once, to buy a silk dress in a sale. There was Mr Wilson's shop where he dealt with stamps and books. M&S hadn't arrived yet and that shop was Lovells, a quality furniture and carpet shop. After lunchtimes like those it was difficult to get back into the office routine. But we finished at five, joining the girls from Boots and Creasey's on the bus back home.

On Saturdays we'd go dancing at the Channel Island Hotel, St George's Hall or Mont au Nord. Live local bands were joined later by the big bands. So soon after the Second World War military bands still thrived. Our dancing partners were often Naval officers. On a weekday, if you saw a Navy boat anchored at sea, as you gazed out of the bus, you knew there'd be a lively Saturday in store. If the Army boys came over you'd be a bit more wary. And if they all came over at the same time my father issued dire warnings about what time I came home, and who with!

Once I met a French Navy officer and we had coffee at the fashionable Maison Carré coffee shop. That was the Moore's Hotel of today. Another time, with two friends, we agreed to take three army boys to see the island. We took the evening bus to L'Ancresse and walked in the sand. We sat in empty boats and talked about our lives. We strolled to the Bridge and they took the bus back to town. There was nothing to fear.

Sometimes after work, we would go to The Shamrock Café and have some coffee. Buddy Holly was the star then, singing 'I guess it doesn't matter anymore'. And Pat Boone with 'Friendly Persuasion', Tommy Steele and 'Singing the Blues' and the Everly Brothers.The Shamrock was very trendy, with its jukebox and Fifties furniture. The best spot was the window where you could see everyone coming and going.

The little town of St Peter Port had a wonderful vitality. You knew everyone and their families. Often you'd know which school people had been to, where they lived and who they married.

Coming home from town you left behind the world of offices and machines. The finance sector had yet to arrive. Most Guernsey people grew, built or fished for a living. There was more land, fewer cars and a strong community. We still lived life close to the seasons and the weather.

I left the *Guernsey Press* to live in England for a while. In 1961 I joined Tektronix, the first industrial company to make a major change to Guernsey's economy. "Tek" introduced locals to a life other than they had ever known before: light industry, personnel departments, a new way of running offices entirely. Whether it has been a good thing, we judge for ourselves. Happily, the *Guernsey Press* is still going strong and I still love words and pictures!

And there is part of Guernsey that will live forever. *Plus ça change, plus c'est la même chose.* The more things change, the more they stay the same. We just have to remember our roots, hold on to our island way of life and ride the waves.

25 Bohemia

September 2001

Whether to rent videos on a Sunday or not? Some years ago just going to the pictures was a bit of fun. On a warm Saturday afternoon my brother and I walked to the North Cinema. This was for children's club. There was a cowboy film on: Roy Rogers with Trigger, his horse. First you watched a 'B' film and a cartoon. Then there might be a newsreel. After the interval came the main feature. We liked anything with Burt Lancaster, Kirk Douglas and Charlton Heston.

My favourite was Doris Day and my sister's was Vera Ellen. Inside the cinema were all our friends, laughing and shouting. When the film broke down, several times, we'd stamp our feet and shout out to the projectionist to hurry up. Cigarette smoke wafted through the beam of light and we tucked into our bags of sweets.

And, before our time, you could get into the North for sixpence including the entry fee, a bar of creamy toffee and a bottle of pop. When people finished their pop, they'd roll the empty bottles under their seats. As the North was built on a slope, you could hear the clink and roll of bottles until they met with a crash at the bottom of the screen.

Then the film could begin. The goodies always won, and the hero or heroine was always in a deathly period at the end of each Saturday showing. 'Will he be saved from the rushing train?' 'Can she escape from the wild gorilla?' To be continued. Of course, they always escaped and survived, but it was always a surprise when we learned just how.

Saturday evenings we'd get dressed up, with pink lipstick and 'California Poppy' scent from Woollies. Walking there and back under moonlit skies we could see the lights of Town sparkling along the St Peter Port coastline.

When we got to the cinema the boys would already be there, bagging the back seats. As the girls came in they'd wolf-whistle and we'd pretend not to notice. Before the film began we'd hear the paso doble, a Latin American marching tune, which the North never changed. At the interval we trooped out to the corner shop to get chocolates, but really to show off our outfits. Gangs of boys would park their motorcycles near the

Tony and Yvonne Ozanne,
Bohemians

shop and call out to us. I got my first kiss, fleeting, aged 13, from one of them. He later married a teacher. I've never forgotten it, but I can't remember what film we saw.

The Gaumont was the second best cinema. One day we went to see 'Gone with the Wind'. At the interval we queued up to get an ice-cream from the uniformed usherette.

We had already bought some Treets from The Chocolate Box and the lady with the glossy, red lipstick and gold jewellery. By the time we blinked into the daylight of St Julian's Avenue our cheeks were streaked with tears, 'Frankly, my dear, I don't give a damn,' said Clark Gable. Oh, poor Vivien Leigh. On the bus home we could hardly bear the sadness. What a film.

But, if you had a boyfriend, and he'd bought tickets for the Odeon, the front balcony, and it was a Sunday night, and he gave you chocolates – you were considered to be practically engaged. This was serious stuff. Holding hands on the picture bus back home was just about tolerated. We'd gaze at these couples, all in their best, and sigh.

Television had just come to Guernsey. Our Uncle Jack was the first to buy one. We were allowed to ride our bikes over on a Sunday evening to see Quatermass, which was absolutely terrifying. People fell into pits and were threatened by alien forces.

Sometimes we'd see the BBC news, only one BBC channel and no ITV, let alone Sky. This was very formal. There was a globe turning with a message going around it saying 'Nation shall speak peace onto nation' with sombre music. We sat to attention until the end. When the evening's viewing was finished we had to wait until the National Anthem had been played and a nice picture of the Queen was shown. We liked the one of her on her horse best.

By the time we went home it was dark. I had borrowed my great-uncle Alf's bike; it was quite big with a crossbar. My auntie, with the television, was worried about us travelling home in the dark lanes. 'I'll give you all cigarettes. Light them and hold them in your hand. Strangers will think you're men.'

And so it was. I rode home, wobbling, on great-uncle Alf's crossbarred bike, puffing a cigarette, still shaking from Quatermass, but we got home safely.

For another entertainment we began to go to junior dances. At the Hermitage Hotel we learned waltzes and foxtrots, the Gay Gordons and the Valetta.

All cousins, we danced with each other. Gradually rock 'n' roll came about. If you danced to Bill Haley's 'Rock Around the Clock' the room would spin and you'd be out of breath. Later at St George's Hall, Syd James brought over big bands like Sid Phillips, Ted Heath, and the Squadronaires.

The Channel Islands Hotel, the Royal Hotel and the Mont au Nord all became popular. As we entered our teens you might hold a party dance, say four of you, and have a theme. There were pyjama and Bohemian parties, always a live, local band.

Then, with rock 'n' roll and the twist and jive took over. As the '50s ended things changed. They were changing all around us. More cars, the end of rationing. In 1963 The Beatles played at Candie Gardens, where we had been many times with my mother. If it rained drips fell on to you from the glass roof. We saw Ken Dodd, the Kaye Sisters and many good vaudeville concerts. Videos on a Sunday? In our time we knew what Sunday was for. But we had such fun. Maybe the two went together.

26 Sweethearts

November 2003

These days young people can court by Internet. You 'post' your photograph and details on the website, (a worldwide computer address). You can exchange e-mails (which is electronic mail, like telephone calls but printed on computer screen, and called 'e-mail' for short) with someone for weeks, months even before you meet. So, when you do meet you already know a lot about each other. Except, of course, whether the love is there, and whether this is the one you want to spend cold Winter nights with.

Those were the days, when courting meant holding hands, a light kiss on the cheek, a knowing look of the love with the eyes – and that was all. All the delights of love were yet to come. That's what was called romance.

There was a modesty in our day. Young men wanted their future wife to be chaste. They'd come calling in their best suits, collar and tie. The girls would have spent ages, applying makeup from Woollies and Boots Number Seven 'Cherry Ripe' liptstick and Gala 'Heavenly Pink'. We set our hair with Amami lotion, or had it permed. We'd backcomb our hair and spray it with sticky lacquer from a plastic bottle. Sunbathing gave us lovely tans which we compared with much competition. Our glamourous screen heroines were Doris Day, Vivien Leigh and Lauren Bacall. Stiff net petticoats were all the rage then, and coming back as this year's fashion.

A lot of our summer courting was done on country walks, taking the bus to town, favourite spots on the beach and, in the winter at dances. There were novelty dances and all the main hotels had variety shows. Wallers, Studio Story, Happy Snaps and Quayside Studio all sent photographers around the bays and hotels and town. The photographer gave you a numbered ticket and you went to collect your photograph from their shops in town.

At the Channel Islands Hotel, St Georges Hall and church social clubs a boy would ask you to dance. He might have had to cross the dance floor and if you said "No", he had to walk all the way back. Often you saw

Pyjama party, 1960

boys you knew from school, from your parish or friends of cousins. Once the last dance was played, usually a waltz, you partnered up. Knowing your curfew would be around eleven at night, he would walk you home or take you home on the picture bus. He might ask you for a date, and your courtship began.

When divorce was unheard of, living together only began after marriage, a courtship followed a strict pattern. Your young man was introduced to your parents. If they approved you went out together to the pictures, and dance halls. If he started taking you to the Odeon on a Sunday night and gave you chocolates, you could start saving for a trousseau. Holding hands was now okay in public and soon after that showing off your engagement ring. Nearly all of us were engaged by twenty-five.

We never went off the island on holiday together. That was unheard of. Those who did had to pretend to be married and bought cheap gold rings. It was thought quite seedy to have a 'dirty weekend'.

You had a, sometimes, quite simple and not always white wedding, but it was always in church. Often there'd be no honeymoon and you had saved up for a deposit and mortgage on a house. A year or so after that babies arrived. That was marriage.

But I remember a few girls getting pregnant outside of marriage. They were kept indoors for the whole nine months. Sometimes the baby was passed off as their mother's or an aunt's child. The stigma of illegitimacy was very hard. If you had a boyfriend and you got pregnant you almost always *had* to get married before the baby was born. The father was expected to support you and your child. Yet I know very many of these marriages were successful, happy and long-lasting.

My father had a list of boys we were not allowed to court: Italians, because of what he thought that country had done during the Second World War; Germans, for the same reason. Anyone who was the son of a Guernsey woman who had fraternised with young German soldiers. Any boy who wasn't white (he had had some bad experiences whilst in the RAF in India) and generally anyone who wasn't a Guernseyman and not from the Vale! My intended was from the Forest but my father-in-law and father were both tomato growers and shared a liking of the same whisky. So that was alright.

Years later I pointed out to Dad that many Italians in Guernsey had done very well for themselves, owning restaurants and hotels. But he never changed his mind. One of our uncles, in his late sixties, fell in love with his brother's wife. For years he visited them socially, all the while loving Clemmie secretly. But there was absolutely no question of infidelity. One day the much respected brother died. My uncle moved in with Clemmie. They shared the same surname and were together until their eighties, when she died. My uncle said the years with her had been the best in his life and he died a happy man.

But, now, a strange thing has happened. The ancient art of formal courtship has returned for Internet dating. After 'talking' to each other on the computer for a while couples meet. They might go for a drink, but with other friends. Then, maybe, they might have dinner with nothing more than a kiss on the cheek and a promise to meet again. After a time of this old-fashioned wooing the pair may go on to spend a night together and even marry.

So the human need for love and companionship hasn't dimmed. Flirtation and the gentle art of wooing survives. Perhaps, all those years ago, as we strolled hand in hand in our pretty Guernsey lanes, sipped coffee in town and glanced shyly at each other as we sat on a beach, sharing a towel, we got it right, after all.

Long live romance.

27 *Luton Hats*

March 2006

William Morris Russell died on February 16th, 2006. Who was he? Well, with his partner Peter Hobbs, Mr Russell was the inventor of the Russell Hobbs electric kettle.

We were given both a Russell Hobbs electric kettle *and* a Russell Hobbs coffee percolator as wedding presents. In our day (late Fifties and early Sixties), with these two elegantly designed items we could claim to be a thoroughly modern couple (for the first and last time.) Not only that, we received a set of Prestige cooking utensils (which I use to this day).

It was either a lovely white wedding or a honeymoon, not both. So, after the ceremony we travelled back to Luton, Bedfordshire, where we rented a flat. Tony worked for the Rootes Group and I, Vauxhall Motors. So our one week's honeymoon was spent in Luton – just at the time when, for the British, a holiday in Jersey was all the rage! The 'Merton Hotel' ran honeymoon specials (becoming known as 'The Honeymoon Hotel') and Jersey began to be called 'the island of love'.

Luton was a town so involved in car production that its people joked they might as well say 'Luton, near to Vauxhall' since whole families and generations found employment there. The 'Luton van' is called that because a former thriving industry had been straw hat making (Luton Town football team, based at Kenilworth Road get their nickname 'The Hatters' because of this.)

When transporting hats they were stored upright and over the van cab – thus the Luton vans became their famous shape. Also, the 'Bedford' lorry is called that after the capital of Bedfordshire.

The photograph shows Tony, second from right, with his Luton friends on holiday in Guernsey. They are wearing straw hats, much in demand that year, 1958, when Luton Town FC were in the Cup Final.

Coming as I did from our green and beautiful island, Luton came as a bit of a culture shock. Tony had already been living there for eight years. I took quite some time to adjust: the grass in the parks was greasy from the then permitted black smoke pouring all day from factory chimneys. You had to be quick on your pins when you boarded double-decker buses since they barely stopped for passengers. But I became fascinated by the trains and of how quickly you could get up to London.

Tony Ozanne with Luton friends, 1958

That was a plus point – going to up to London. We went to hear the American jazz pianist, Errol Garner, and, in the interval, found a quiet place for a coffee. Right opposite us sat Shirley Bassey with her then husband. I didn't dare ask for an autograph. She was impossibly elegant and tiny, yet seemed to fill the space around her, more even than the pianist star we had all come to hear.

The film 'A Kind of Loving' with Alan Bates and June Ritchie was shown in 1962. It still reminds me of living in Luton. I looked a bit like June Ritchie then and was almost as naïve as her character of 'Ingrid'. The story was set in a Northern town, but it was very like Luton in those days: grey rain, sooty net curtains.

In the lunchtimes at Vauxhall factory they sometimes had live acts. I remember Adam Faith 'Wadd do ya wan if ya donne wan money? Wadd do ya wan if ya donne wan love?' I was ecstatic to see him in the very flesh. But my colleagues were less than impressed, shrugging nonchalantly that they had seen him before.

A novelty for me was having our own canteen at Vauxhall, with subsidised prices. It was interesting. Though there were three canteens: the shop floor workers, us, the office workers and 'the management'. And 'the management' had their own toilet facilities. They had cloths on their tables and stainless steel cruet sets, whereas we had washable plastic tables and the salt and pepper pots were in plain glass and nearly always damp.

In our department (typing up endless orders for components) – you were paid by the word. Lunchtimes were staggered because of the vast numbers. We had the 'Starvation Break' – 2.30-3.00pm. But the food was excellent. I liked Wednesdays because it was Lancashire hotpot and treacle pudding with custard. I can still taste these delicious treats.

But in time, exactly as with our decimated growing industry, native British car manufacturing industry collapsed. This devastated the Midlands. We knew how they felt, we had witnessed the beginning of the end of our own horticultural way of life.

Just then, the American producers of oscilloscopes, Tektronix Inc., wanted a base in Europe. They chose Guernsey. We left Luton and returned home. Although I had missed so much: my family, the glorious beaches and our fresh, clean air I was sorry to leave the Luton people we had come to know. We are still in close touch with many friends. The true Luton person is a doughty soul, plain speaking and with pioneer spirit. Maybe that's why we all liked each other?

William Russell and Peter Hobbs, manufacturers themselves, left an iconic image with their Kettle (K1). Yet they, too, saw great changes in their time. By 1963 they sold their company and Russell Hobbs is now under American ownership.

Vauxhall Motors is owned by the American company, General Motors and now Tektronix is USA based. I like to think, though, through collective memory, our individual efforts in the workplace have counted. Luton has changed. My Vauxhall office (and the factory with it), has now been raised to the ground. Many Luton people moved out of the Town centre and into outlying places like Harlington, Dunstable and Milton Keynes.

Guernsey now has a prestigious, enviable Finance Sector. We are fortunate that this is so. Without the growing industry and a less robust tourist sector, a healthy economic system would not be possible. Guernsey must pay for everything: its own education, health and pension schemes etc. Now, we have to be like William Russell – entrepreneurs as our ancestors were: innovative, resourceful and strong. Because life, after all, goes on come what may and we have to change to survive.

28 French Connection
May 2003

On May 1st my son-in-law's book, *Laws of Guernsey*, is published. Guernsey is about to celebrate eight hundred years of its status as a near independent jurisdiction. Gordon's remarkable book is the first exposition of Guernsey law for 250 years. Our, vital, historical links with Normandy are made clear.

I lived in Normandy for six months. My daughter and her husband, a solicitor and barrister, needed to study at Caen University in order to qualify as Guernsey Advocates. I was nanny to my two granddaughters, then aged two and a half and four years.

Whilst the students went off to Caen every day, I remained in Ouistreham where we had rented a house. The first few weeks were in turn lonely and difficult. I had little French. But every morning I took the children to a small village school in neighbouring Lion-sur-Mer.

Very gradually something quite odd happened. I started to recognise things. Once the girls were settled I began to explore Lion-sur-Mer. I had fallen in love with this little village, set by a long sandy beach. As I walked around the sunny church square, bells peeling, and bought some fresh bread, people began to acknowledge me. I truly felt as though I must have been here before. I felt so at home. But it was the home of my childhood, fifty years and more ago.

This feeling kept happening. "Hello Claude!" I called to an old man, wheeling his bike, cigarette in the corner of his mouth. But Claude, my late father-in-law, has been dead these past fourteen years! Three women, sitting on a seawall, chattering and laughing together, could have been my sisters. In the narrow high street two older people, wrapped up against the cold wind, stared into the window of a Charcuterie. They were arguing about whether to buy a cooked lobster. Their patois and way they spoke to each other, "Ah, weh," one of them said (not "oui,") sounded just like my great uncle and aunt when I was young.

Many of our names, like Delamare and Bréhaut, are found in Normandy. One day, feeling a bit alone, I explored a leafy country lane. I was headed toward the Chateau in Lion-sur-Mer. Just then, a white van rattled toward me. On the side of the van were the words, 'B. Heaume. Plombier. Ouistreham'. So, there was even a plumber, with my grandmothers' name, alive and well in Normandy! I smiled, all the way home.

Throughout the bitterly cold early months of 2000, Lion-sur-Mer infant school held all kinds of events. At a 'Spectacle', held in a Salle (village hall), the children had their school concert. As parents and grandparents found their seats, talking French loudly, laughing and proudly watching their children, we stopped feeling like strangers. We were offered wine and home made cakes and sat on long tables as the children ran around freely. It was like being in the parish hall of my youth, for a Sunday school outing. I half expected Great Aunt Elise to walk in. She would have been given a chair and found herself perfectly at home. The older generation is still revered, houses kept in the family, tradition respected.

These Norman people were well, but by no means all fashionably dressed. There were no Range Rovers parked outside. Indeed, most had walked from their homes and were utterly at ease with themselves.

That is not to say that Lion-sur-Mer is a backwater. Not a bit of it. The little school had state of the art computers. Modern technology is highly regarded. There is an air of curiosity, of wanting to be informed, but the traditional way of doing things is still valued.

As I got to know the village, I observed scenes as if from my past. A man in a small courtyard washed his hands in a white enamel basin, set on tripod. It was just like the one we had, kept in our outside washhouse. The man poured water from a china jug. His dog sat in the sun on a wicker chair, watching him.

Another time an elderly man, in black braces, shirt sleeves rolled up, prepares his lunch on a table outside in a small backyard. All around are pots of geraniums. His kitchen door is left ajar and I can smell the haricot beans and onions of a cassoulet. On the checked cloth he sets out bread, cheese and a half filled bottle of red wine.

Further down the hill, opposite the church, a large lady has set her table on the pavement, outside her terraced house. Pots of flowers spill down some stone steps. Her friends interrupt their shopping to stop and wish her good morning. They talk to her as she slices some garlic sausage and pours wine from a brown jug. Other people pass by with their bread and fresh cakes from the shop next door. All is unhurried and civilised.

From the window of our rented house we can see the whole stretch of

Ouistreham bay, looking like a very wide Vazon. Every day, rain or shine, people collected mussels, washed up in their thousands, a seashore of blue shells. I am reminded of my mother, cockling at L'Islet. Bikes are parked on the sea wall at the top of the beach. Sometimes a baguette is tied to them and people, full bags in hand, go off to cook their breakfast.

Ouistreham, Normandy, France

The French village school

In Caen University Guernsey's Norman law is taught. Our very roots are here. I am excited to see the city of my ancestors' culture – where our way of life comes from. And it is a living history, with William the Conqueror's stronghold, his castle, still standing. He is buried in the Cathedral Abbaye aux Hommes, Caen.

Back in Ouistreham, I take the children to see the open air fish market, set on the harbour. Huge live lobsters, crabs and lady crabs vie for space.

There are mussels, oysters, cockles and winkles set on ice with lemons and parsely. The locals queue in the cold and wet to buy their supper. I buy some mackerel and weep for our market and what has happened to it.

The courteous French kiss upon greeting each other. I remember the gentility of my great uncles and aunts, their modesty and ordered way of life. I never thought I would see their like again. But they are to be found in Normandy still. Old Guernsey has not been completely lost.

When I left Normandy and Lion-sur-Mer behind I vowed to go back. And I shall. On the last day I picked the children up from the school I looked over the wooden gate. I saw the sturdy old trees in the playground, pollarded short, the French way. Chickens in the meadow next door clucked aimlessly to each other. The men and women I had come to know smiled kindly at me, as they always had. Some took their children home on the crossbars of their bikes. One sweet woman brought a battered pram, for her four year-old, as she always did. These are our relations. These Norman people are our neighbours, content and sure of their way of life.

One look back as I drove away for the last time. I arrived in Guernsey with tears in my eyes for Normandy. We must never sever this living link. Never threaten our island and cut ourselves adrift in hostile seas. For lawyers not to study in Caen would, without question, be the beginning of the end for Guernsey.

It is a threat worse than any war on her. If it ever happens, our children will lose the Guernsey we love and cherish. She will be like any county in England, or the Isle of Wight. But Guernsey is not like any other place on earth. Guernsey is special, Guernsey is Norman French. We must always be prepared for battle against those who wish to deny Guernsey its ancient and remarkable history. And it is a battle we have to win.

108

29 Freddie

May 2004

From a very young age, I remember talk of both the first and second world wars. We didn't understand the significance of these, of course. Yet our parents and all our relations and friends all seemed to have been affected, one way or another.

Mr Churchill seemed to be mentioned a lot, and Monty and King George V1 and Kitchener. And, later, I remember my father talking about Atlee, 'old rat face Gaitskill' (a Labour Prime Minister,) and 'Unflappable Mac' (Harold MacMillan). So there was always an interest in politics in our house.

In 1952, I remember the solemn wireless announcement: "This is the BBC. Ladies and gentlemen, the King is dead. Long live the Queen." Then my mother ran in tears to my great-aunt Elise next door.

Nevertheless, my great-aunt Elise, Norman French and no monarchist, always told me she wouldn't cross the street to see the Queen of England. And when the Queen did come to Guernsey, in 1957, her cavalcade (including Prince Philip) took her around the grassy village green in front of the Vale Church. Close to where we lived, we schoolchildren stood three deep and waved and cheered. But great-aunt Elise didn't budge from Solidor.

Great-aunt Elise never married. She could have, she often told me, but all the young men of her generation were killed in the First World War. She was probably right. Certainly the young man she loved was lost and never returned. "I had a 'site' (boyfriend) you know," she'd say. "Don't think I didn't!"

So the Guernsey men and women who served in the forces were volunteers. Guernsey people, being neither English nor French, were not compulsorily conscripted. 'For King and Country' meant, for our people, our allegiance to the Crown of England, and for Guernsey.

Each family was in some way involved with the wars, those who stayed and those who went. Just thinking of our one Vale family I can count life transforming acts of bravery and endurance. Duncan Bréhaut, my father's younger brother, was a crack rifle shot. He joined the army, Hampshire

Freddie Bréhaut, 1916

Freddie, Mont du Val, 1912

division and was chosen to guard VIP and dangerous prisoners-of-war. He was just a young man in his twenties. My uncle Gerry Torode, my aunty Mary's (née Bréhaut) husband, was an army motorcycle-messenger in France, and was later Mentioned In Dispatches. He had carried out his duties in the teeth of enemy fire and was involved in the D Day Normandy landings. He had undertaken many secret missions, and had seen the killing of many of his friends – none of which he would ever talk about.

My father, Uncles Rex Green, Roy Sheppard, Jack Goubert and Len Willis joined the armed forces. They served in India, Africa, Europe and Britain, leaving their island and families behind for many years. My father joined the RAF and, because he was a boat-owning Guernseyman, was immediately made skipper of an Air Sea Rescue unit in India.

Another uncle, Fred Hockey, escaped in heavy mist by boat from Guernsey to England, to tell the authorities of the horrendous conditions Guernsey people were undergoing.

But the worse loss of all to us, I feel, was of Frederick Bréhaut. He was my grandfather Edwin Bréhaut's younger brother. Having joined the Royal Guernsey Light Infantry, he was killed in France during the Cambrai battle along with thousands of other men.

Frederick was the beloved youngest child of my great-grandparents, Alfred and Nancy (née Duchemin) Bréhaut. Nancy was an Alderney lady.

Frederick was a handsome fair-haired young man, born into, what was considered to be, a quite wealthy family in those days. He had lived the life of a gentleman. "He never worked," said my great aunt Elise, "none of those Bréhaut sons did."

So, Edwin, my grandfather, Alfred junior and Frederick lived a comfortable life in Castel. There was no reason for Frederick to volunteer, save he wanted to 'do his duty'. When Frederick was killed, his identification labels were sent to his parents' home in an envelope.

When his mother opened the letter, the metal tags were still covered in Frederick's dried blood. He died on December 1st, 1917, just before the First World War came to an end. He is buried in Cambrai Memorial Cemetery, France.

Nancy never recovered from her loss and it damaged her health. The family's stonemason and building firm took a downward turn and the Bréhauts later lived quietly and modestly at La Blanche Charrière, Vale, until their deaths.

I wasn't going to write so much about Frederick, but Nancy has had other ideas! Although dead for very many years, she has guided me to finding out more about Frederick: how old he was; where he died and when. I was guided to the Spencer Museum, Castle Cornet, where there is a marvellous Militia Museum. They show details of all the Guernsey losses, with photographs and maps of Cambrai and Ribecourt. "My Frederick is not going to be forgotten," she seemed to be saying to me.

Nor should any of our islanders be forgotten. Not those who served, those who were wounded, those who died, those who were deported and those who stayed and lived under pitiful conditions until they were liberated.

Frederick Bréhaut was 26 years old when he died. What a waste of life. But then, wars are all about waste. The motto of the Royal Guernsey Light Infantry was 'Dieux Aix' – 'God Help Us'.

Now it is a time of Liberation, 60 years of freedom and 800 years of independence. Now, we can think of all those men and women who, with God's help, kept our island free for us. And, now, we owe them all a very great deal.

30   Remember, Remember

November 2006

November is red with fire, poppies and Beaujolais. As we enter the months of winter and the Christmas season, with darkened evenings and winter cold, we brighten a night or two with bonfires and fireworks. When Guernsey people were more in touch with the seasons, the end of a productive year, following harvest would be celebrated by burning a Yule log, *le bout d'lan*. The Guernsey patois words have, over the years, morphed into 'Budlo'. Literally, they mean *bout* – the butt end – *d'lan* – of the year.

Before the 1914-18 war private fireworks parties were almost unknown. But the notorious war and flood of young soldiers' blood, slain at Flanders, began our red poppy day. Now, on Remembrance Day, we remember all men and women of both world wars and of all battles fought for our sakes. I cannot watch the ceremony at the Cenotaph with dry eyes. The moving sight of older men and women, some simply covered in medals for bravery, and the thought of all the young lives lost on foreign fields never fails to bring home how dearly we must treasure our peace.

The red poppy is of remembrance, not a celebration of war. White poppies representing peace might have their place, but not on the very day set aside for the loved ones of the Armed Forces who sacrificed their lives and never came back. Wearing a red poppy or not is neither here nor there. The Duchess of Cornwall was criticised for not wearing a red poppy on a recent visit abroad to Pakistan with the Prince of Wales. Yet we saw her recently, clearly moved, visiting the graveside of a relation lost in World War Two. When I lived in France I went to a ceremony where Prince Charles opened a new Pegasus museum for the remembrance of the Red Berets, parachuted in at a crucial early landing – beginning the Allied Landings in Normandy. Prince Charles was, quite obviously, deeply interested in the old servicemen presented to him, knowledgeable and took a long time talking to all of the people individually.

Surely, the last thing these courageous servicemen and women want is obligatory gestures to their actions? They were fighting for freedom and democracy, for goodness sake. Red poppies should be worn by choice and when thought appropriate by the wearer. These individual choices are the cornerstone of our civilization.

Goodbye to the boys, 1917

As we move deeper into winter and begin to plan our Christmas and how to decorate our houses, most of us will put a Christmas tree in pride of place. Maybe we forget that we are continuing the long history of bringing a living tree, the same idea as a Yule log, into our sitting rooms. We decorate the tree with lights – the equivalent of candle flame – and place little glittering decorations on it. Do we even think now, that these silver bells and small, edible treats were once put there to appease the spirits? The idea is similar to Halloween (which I never celebrate – I think this is a time when souls and saints should be left peacefully to themselves), a dark time in our calendar when malign forces might be most meddlesome.

November and December are traditionally the time of year when our western world is darkest, coldest and our crops are hibernating. So hurrah for December 21st, the Winter Solstice when we can celebrate the return of the sun and any mischievous spirits must flee before returning light. As we make garlands of holly, ivy and evergreens we reflect, albeit sometimes unknowingly, our belief in regeneration and resurrection.

On our bonfire night – originating from 'bone fire' when animal bones were disposed of as fuel: lending heat and light to chilled mortals – we warm ourselves. We make nourishing food and say goodbye to poor old Guy Fawkes, whose effigy who has been burnt so ceremoniously and, probably, erroneously, all these years.

This year we lit our small bonfire and set off a modest selection of fireworks – mainly for our granddaughter's benefit. And from childhood I remember Bonfire Night being more about the bonfire than the fireworks. But I don't have a good track record of bonfire nights. I remember getting burnt by a Catherine wheel when about five, never did like all the noise and I went into false labour 39 years ago (my son should have been born November 12th under Scorpio, an excellent entrepreneur sign, but he hung on until November 24th). So Michael is a Sagittarius, a hugely creative, larger than life sign and yes, he is both. And my mother, Mary Bréhaut, is 87 and not out, today the 25th). Our West Highland terrier, Frazer, barks so much at the bangs of fireworks (are they much louder and more powerful than they used to be? Whatever happened to nice, fizzy 'Golden Fountains'?) that we have been driven to give him tranquillisers. Since around our way Guy Fawkes day goes on from the 1st until anything up to 8th of November, Frazer has spent quite some time quietly sozzled and looking quite bewildered.

So now it is time to look forward to the wonderful traditional Christian celebration of Christmas, and the New Year. Our poultry, meats and fish are ordered. Efficient cooks will have made their rich fruitcakes and plum puddings, chutneys and bottled fruits – yet more traditional symbols of plenty and of feasting to carry us through. Families begin to make arrangements so they know where they will be together on December 25th and January 1st. It is not so long after that when Guernsey's early spring, that we are so fortunate to enjoy, arrives. For now, we light our warming fires, prepare our comfort food and remember all those who are no longer with us, but whose lives have so enriched us and they will never be forgotten.

31 Of Gentle Nobility

October 2006

May I generalize? There is in the face of the Guernsey man an honesty and quiet strength that is quite unique. You can see this determination and direct gaze in the *Guernsey Press* photographs taken at the Swimarathon (which raised an astounding one million pounds.) Incidentally, The Barracudas swam for an amazing 24 hours (2,280 laps). School children of all ages and abilities were encouraged by their schools to take part. Even Beau Sejour's life guards joined in on their time off. In all some 176 teams, and 1,336 swimmers took part. This is one more remarkable but unsurprising example of islanders' vigorous community spirit.

And the Guernseyman's natural decency is conveyed every time the *Flying Christine* is called out, sometimes in atrocious conditions, or when charity is asked for. I have been reading about Guernsey resident, Dr Roger Allsop's Channel swim with unsurprised but huge admiration. Dr Allsop raised £15,000 for a cancer research project. He could not have done it, he said, "without the support of the people of Guernsey." But he alone braved challenging weather conditions for an astounding 15 and and a half hours.

Through television we could witness a similar struggle that Dr Allsop must have endured when we followed the programme showing David Walliams, the comedian, also swimming the Channel. How cold and rough the water seemed with the sea full of filthy debris and strong currents. France must have seemed an awful long way off. Dr Allsop said he felt sick at the start but he battled on. What a tremendous feat of courage. I would even be loath to swim to Herm like we did in our younger days, never mind all the way to St Malo.

Guernsey people have a time-honoured history not only connected with the sea but of giving time and money for all kinds of charity. No wonder Victor Hugo called us 'noble little people' and Guernsey 'the rock of hospitality and liberty; that corner of old Normandy soil where dwells that noble little people of the sea. To the island of Guernsey, austere yet gentle'. Spot on Victor. And, more lyrically, he also described our islands as 'fragments of France which fell into the sea and were picked up by England'. And we have always felt more a little piece of France than England.

Years later when we were liberated from Nazi occupation, the great Winston Churchill warmed out hearts by calling us 'the dear Channel Islands.' These expressions by Hugo and Churchill, of a rooted, grounded people, fair and dark, Norman or Breton, can still apply to Guernsey men and women. I am writing here about the men mostly, but I know Guernseywomen will bear with me and know why. There is a fraternity amongst Guernseymen – still noticeable with both young and old – of good humoured frankness which is heart-warming.

Castle swim, 1920s

Years ago, Inter-Insular swimming Galas were held at Havelet in Guernsey. The Inter-Insular sports games are a strong part of our culture and it is good to see these competitions still running. But, and it doesn't diminish swimmers' achievements one bit, to say that they are held in far warmer, cleaner conditions than in the old days. The outdoor sea water swimming pools were bracing at best and freezing at worst. Still, a lot of fun was had by both competitors and spectators alike. I can remember sitting on the hard boulders round the pools, yelling for the Guernsey team with the sea-breeze whipping up waves and chilling our cheeks.

As for the Castle swim (from Castle Cornet to the Havelet bathing pools) – again, this was entered into with gusto and keen rivalry: another instance of Guernsey people using their sea with good nature and friendliness. These qualities are still with us. We see them in the young men serving in garages; the butchers, builders and workmen all around our island. Yes, and in the finance sector: banks and offices. Every shop and supermarket has Guernseymen serving – unassuming with a kind of secure confidence. (All right. I did say I was generalizing.)

Watch any local football team, talk to any boatmen and you will see the Guernsey open spirit and belief in himself. This strength of character and clarity of purpose is what gives us our unique community. It is very distinct and we can take immense pride in it. Heavens, what mainland Britain right now would give for this kinship.

Our 'noble little people' – our rock, have taken the sea that surrounds us and dealt with it respectfully. We have used it and enjoyed it, with events like the parish regattas. This year we enjoyed wonderful seafood under marquees overlooking our harbour. The scene could not have been be bettered in any St Tropez or far flung glamorous port.

Why on earth would we want a 'Little Venice'? Scale down the proposed development and call it 'Petite Belle Grèves' ('Lovely little sandy beaches') and we might, at least, give the idea consideration.

Our forebears looked after Guernsey well. In turn, the surrounding sea has protected our beautiful island all these years and kept us special. For this is our very own green and pleasant land. Let us guard it jealously, for doesn't charity begin at home?

32 George

On June 28th 1940, a month before his twentieth birthday and on a day that promised glorious sunshine, 'Young George Bréhaut' as he was known, set off in his lorry to pick up tomato chips for Mr Frederick Vaudin's customers. George would take the loaded lorry for store packing and then the White Rock and park it in a queue, ready for the cargo boat next day. Sometimes the queue was very long so it was important to get in place early.

But, as fate would have it, having worked, collecting his load all day that by that sunny and peaceful evening, George Bréhaut, a civilian, was killed by a German bullet. For George was one of around thirty Guernsey people who were callously and deliberately annihilated on the White Rock harbour at the beginning of the enemy occupation of our island. The Nazis' main objective, with their *Operation Grune Pfeile* (Green Arrow), had been merely to ascertain how defended Guernsey was. So the line of lorries and vans, some horse drawn, packed with tomato chips and ready for departure, were bombed.

For nearly an hour everyone on the St Peter Port harbour, some three hundred totally unarmed and exposed people – men, women and children – were subjected to the bombing. Even clearly marked St John Ambulances, the Guernsey lifeboat and fishermen in their little open boats were targeted and fired at.

Many people were waiting for embarkation to England on the mail steamer *Isle of Sark* which had only light anti-aircraft guns. By chance the tide was low so some terrified souls could rush to safety under the piers. Otherwise the toll of death (31) would undoubtedly have been much higher. As it was, many lorry drivers who had dived under their vehicles were killed as petrol tanks caught fire and they were burned alive.

George Bréhaut shouldn't have even been on the White Rock that day. Let Mr Desmond Vaudin tell you his story:

My father Mr Frederick Vaudin, was a tomato packer and carter who

German bomb, White Rock, St Peter Port Harbour, Guernsey, 1940

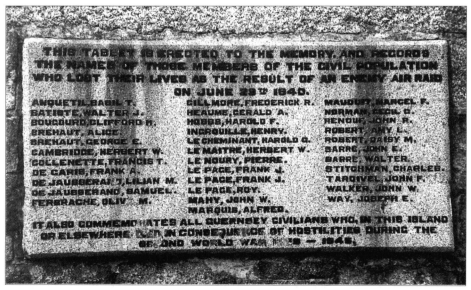

In honour of those slain, 1940

had just started his new business in 1939. He owned a new Commer lorry and a new Commer van.

One week before the German air raid he suffered an attack of lumbago and was unable to drive his lorry.

One of his grower customers, Mr George Bréhaut, who lived at La Girouette, St Saviours and had an only son – George junior, volunteered his son to help my Dad picking up chips of tomatoes and delivering them to the packing station and then to the harbour all that week. On the Friday I, aged 14, accompanied George junior to help in loading the lorry. George told me that he had seen a German plane flying over, but I did not believe him.

When the time came to go to the White Rock with the load I said it would be pointless my going with him as the procedure was to take the lorry to the back of the queue – which sometimes could go back as far as the Royal Hotel or even Salarie Corner. The lorries were parked for the night, ready to be unloaded the following morning. The Commer van was parked on the White Rock pier and George would come home in it. George took the load at about 5 pm and, after joining the queue and parking the lorry he collected the Commer van to come back home. Just then the Luftwaffe started bombing and strafing the line of lorries. The Commer van was riddled with bullet holes. George Bréhaut junior, the nineteen year old volunteer, was dead.

By sheer co-incidence, a few days after I had received Mr Vaudin's letter, I attended a family occasion in Cambridge. I talked to John and Nina Ogier who I knew had lived at La Girouette.

I asked John if he knew anything about George. It transpired that not only did John remember George Bréhaut junior but he distinctly recalls June 28, 1940. Here is the account of what John remembers:

'Young George' Bréhaut lived with his parents George and Ethel (nee Le Moigne) at 'La Girouette', lower St Saviours. The property was the home of my grandparents, John and Marybell Le Couteur. The Bréhauts rented part of the property known as 'The Old House' which adjoined and interconnected with the main house.

Young George was a lorry driver for the Fruit Export Company (or possibly G. Holmes). I think I remember the colour of his lorry as blue. I was six years-old at the time and had enjoyed rides in George's cab many times.

On the evening of June 28, 1940, my elder brother Bill and I, together with my mother, grandmother and Ethel Bréhaut were seated around the kitchen table. Bill and I were shelling peas and making Spitfires and Messerschmitts with pea pods. We could quite clearly hear the bombardment of the White Rock, six miles away. The adults became anxious as neither my father nor young George had returned from St Peter Port. We worried that what we had heard was perhaps a preliminary aggressive invasion of the whole Island.

Eventually my father, Stanley, returned home. Before taking cover he had watched the arrival of the Heinkel 111 bombers from a window of the National Provincial Bank where he worked. The view from the window was over the harbour.

On his way home he saw an elderly relative, a veteran of the 1914/18 war who had stationed himself behind his garden wall complete with a 12 bore gun and 'ammo' at the ready. He was waiting "For the first Gerry to make an appearance!"

But it was getting late and there was still no sign of Young George. So my father drove back into Town and searched the White Rock. He was a member of the ARP (Air Raid Precaution) and so he was directed to the mortuary and there he found and identified the remains of young George Bréhaut.

After the war we (the Ogiers) moved to the mainland. By then George and Ethel Bréhaut lived in a cottage at L'Arquet, very close to the Mirus Battery. This would have been the summer of 1948."

So, of course, the awful truth of what happened to Young George was finally learned and the Bréhaut family's lives, like so many others on that fine June evening, were never to be the same again.

And five years on, with Liberation as we have been remembering this year, thousands of Guernsey lives – our whole way of life, in fact, was irrevocably changed. Mr Desmond Vaudin wanted those ordinary people on that day like any other, going about their peaceful business to have their place in our history, as well. I agree with him and perhaps we can all think of them and thank God once more for the sixty years of freedom those innocent Guernsey people never got to enjoy.

A MASSACRE OF THE UNDEFENDED
June 28, 1940
June 1948; Died at the White Rock; Cause: War Operations

Name	Age	Occupation	Born
John Robin Renouf	69	Fruit Grower	Vale
Samuel William de Jausserand	66	Agent	St P Port
Lilian M de Jausserand	52		London
Cecil Gaudion Norman	26	Lorry driver	St Peters
George Edward Bréhaut	19	Lorry driver	St. Svs
Harold Griffith le Cheminant	73		St P Port
John Francis Tardivel	67		Jersey
Basil Thomas Anquetil	69	Docker	Alderney
Herbert Walter Cambridge	33		English
Frederick Reginald Gillmore	33	Porter	English
John Ernest Sarre	62	Fruit Grower	Guernsey
Gerald Alfred Heaume	15	Storeman	Guernsey
John William Mahy	49	Fruit Grower	Vale
Francis Thomas Collenette	33	Lorry driver	Castel
Frank John le Page	49	Farmer	Castel
Frank John le Page	19	Farmer	Castel
Roy Frederick Le Page	14		Castel
Henry Ingrouille	62	Lorry driver	St Smpsn
John Washington Walker	41	Master builder	England
Herbert Wonderen Le Maitre	60	Carter	Vale
Alfred Marquis	58	Driver	St Andrews
Charles Stitchman	58	Driver	English
Walter James Batiste	40	Driver	St P Port
Pierre Le Noury	60	Farmer	Castel
Clifford Henry Bougourd	32	Police Constable	St Samp
Marcel Francis Maudit	19	Charcutier	France
Harold F Hobbs	33	Lifeboatman	Guernsey

(Mr Harold Hobbs died at sea on 28th June 1940 off Jersey after the relief lifeboat was fired upon by the Luftwaffe)
(Mr Frank Le Page, Frank John Le Page and Roy Frederick Le Page were father and two sons)
(Mr S de Jausserand and Lilian Jausserand were husband and wife)

Died in the Country Hospital; Cause: War Operations
June 28th 1940

Date	Name	Age	Occupation	Born 1940
June 29	Walter Sarre	28	Lorry driver	St Peters
June 28	Alice Mary Adey (Widow of G. Bréhaut)	81		St P Port
June 28	Olive Mary Vaudin (Wife of H.C. Ferbrache)	33		Forest
June 28	Joseph Edward Way	49	Garage prop.	StP Port
June 28	Daisy May Robert	41		StP Port
June 29	Amy Louise Robert	38		StP Port
June 29	Frank Albert de Garis	32	Farmer	Castel

(Daisy May Robert and Amy Louise Robert were sisters, daughters of Peter Edward Robert and Grace Anne Snell)

33   Liberation Day

April 2005

How young they all were, those Guernsey people who endured occupation, evacuation and, for some, deportation. When relations talked of 'during the war', it all seemed so far away, so long ago and, to young people they were all *so old* ! Of course, now, I realise that those thousands of men and women had their very *young* lives torn apart. People in their twenties, thirties and forties had any plans and hopes for university, travel or making a home and raising a family completely disrupted for five years. It seems too awful to contemplate now.

But they came through it. My father-in-law, Claude Ozanne, stayed in Guernsey and coped. Although he kept his house and land he had to join a kind of co-operative where all labour and produce was pooled and shared. Apart from the Red Cross letters that were allowed, heavily censored, he had no contact with his wife and two sons.

My mother-in-law went to Nantwich with my husband Tony, then aged four and her eldest son, Michael, 11. They had to set up a new life until they could return to the island. When they did unite, Tony was nine, Michael 16, Claude 44 and my mother in law, Kath, 42. It is only now one realises that the Ozanne couple were only in their early forties – in the middle of what we now regard as the 'prime time' of life. And that is how it was for thousands more.

Although Guernsey was freed in 1945, the first Liberation Day Cavalcade was held on 9th May 1946. Huge crowds turned out and the band of the Royal Marines wearing their white helmets led the parade. There were the Elizabeth College cadets in khaki and people in gay costumes riding on horseback.

We stood on the grass verge at the Halfway, on the sea side of the road. Float after decorated float passed us by and we all waved and cheered. I didn't realize then what the cavalcade was for or what it signified. But I remember my mother helping me to chose things to wear in red, white and blue and it was a real occasion. People were still dressed in quite dark colours, especially the men and many wore Trilby hats or caps.

125

Michael, Claude, Tony, Kath Ozanne reunited, 1946

Claude Ozanne in occupied Guernsey

126

After so many years of drabness: grey and neutral painted houses and the few cars (all black) – the Liberation Cavalcade was a chance for us to have a bit of fun. There was colourful excess, just for once. Used to rationing and being careful of every bit of food we ate and clothes we wore (things were still darned and bought too big for 'growing into') it was like being at an island-wide party.

I could tell people were very happy and wanted to show their relief and their thanks to all the services: the Army, Navy and Air Forces, the volunteers, nurses and the Red Cross and Salvation Army. The floats were decorated with bunting and Union Jacks and were garlanded with flowers. Our Guernsey flag – the red Cross of St George with the golden cross of Normandy superimposed – hadn't been invented yet but it was quite clear that this was *our* day, our very own Liberation Day.

Since my birthday, May 10th, was so close to the Liberation day holiday I always felt a special pleasure in the Island day off. Indeed, my mother has always maintained that although the day of liberation was May 9th, the actual signing of the surrender on board the British destroyer *Bulldog* was May 10th. Perhaps she was right and I was entitled to just a little extra excitement.

The Cavalcade passed by, and to my delight I caught a red camellia as girls on the floats threw flowers to the crowds. My father said that I could keep it and I treasured the flower until it fell apart.

To me, as a very young child, Britain seemed so far away and France was even further. Guernsey wasn't 'English' and it wasn't 'Europe'. I liked to fill in coupons from the newspaper for holidays in Butlins so that I could get a 'brochures' in the post. I would fill in 'Channel Islands' where it said 'Country' feeling how different and special we were.

My mother told me off when all the brochures arrived, saying that we were certainly not going on holiday to Butlins! For one thing, we had holidays in Guernsey and for another it was quite expensive, even for a holiday camp. And why would we want to go to a holiday camp when we had lovely beaches all around us? But I had just wanted the post to be for me and carried on filling in all kinds of coupons, carefully writing 'Channel Islands' with great satisfaction.

It didn't occur to me that British people mostly confused us with Jersey. And Jersey was just as foreign to me as the main lands, anyway. But as the visitors arrived each summer, delighted with Guernsey and telling us how lucky we were to be living here the sense of being different and better increased.

Later in my life I made friends with young English people who *had* had holidays in Butlins and thoroughly enjoyed them. They told me about the family entertainment laid on: how they went specially prepared for the fancy dress competitions and of the heated swimming pools and live entertainment. How I envied them!

In 1946 the States of Guernsey rejected plans for a Butlins at L'Erée. Maybe it's not too late to rethink the idea? If not an actual Butlins, a well planned holiday complex might be a good thought? Now that we have so little for the tourists who have become used to sophisticated holidays, maybe Guernsey could offer even more than its undoubted beauty and charm? It would be nice to see our visitors back again and in the numbers that they used to come.

As for Liberation Day and the entertainment then laid on for us all to enjoy. Well, it was a wonderful family outing. We knew nearly everyone around us. The whole island celebrated. Crowds stretched either side of us on both sides of the road all the way into Town. The island was united: those who had endured the Occupation; those who had served abroad and those who were evacuated. Guernsey was ours again at long last.

This year, for Liberation Day 2005, a lot of people have worked very hard and a great deal of imagination has gone in to giving us the Sixty Years of Liberation celebration. We are joining together once again in giving thanks for our way of life and for a chance to show how much we love this indomitable isle and how proud we are of her history.

Our Queen, as Duke of Normandy, and Prince Philip are coming to mark the importance of our freedom. We look to Guernsey's future with the courage and determination all Guernsey people have inherited. As we unite and show the world what our island is made of, then nothing has been lost.

34 Shadow to Sunshine

(Title taken from Jurat John Leale's speech May 23, 1945.
A report of five years German Occupation of Guernsey.)

Bertie Le Prevost was 32 when the Second World War began. When peace was declared and the German Occupation of Guernsey was over, Guernsey had been isolated for five years. This is the story of how Bertie survived isolation and loneliness, of his fears that he had lost the love of his life forever. And this is for Guernsey people, for all islanders, an independent people for 800 years. What an island, what a race.

Sighing, Bertie went out and found some twigs. They were damp. He dried them out as best he could on his jumper, set them criss-crossed on the dank, bare hearth and lit them. A thin smoke curled up the chimney. He did all his cooking, now, on the living room fire. Bertie got his empty saucepan and shallow-filled it with water from the tap. He cleaned a cabbage, cut it carefully into four pieces and put some of it to cook. The rest would be for tomorrow and the next day. The day had been grey and foggy – Guernsey at its least attractive. Evening descended and Bertie could hear not a sound from outside. He drew the curtains and put on another jumper. It was so cold. There was no gas or electricity. They had been gone since Christmas. It was the end of April and still with a nip in the air.

Bertie ate his cabbage with some stale bread and a little skimmed milk. He would wash up the dishes after lunch tomorrow, so as to save water. He had a bit of soap he had managed to buy, many months ago, which did for all his cleaning, including himself. Then, there was nothing else to do but go to bed. As he lay there alone, Bertie started to think again of Rita. How beautiful she was. How on earth had he managed to land Rita Tostevin? She was top drawer stuff, her, a real lady. What the hell would she make of him once she came back to Guernsey with their little Rose? As he lay there, a tear ran down his thin cheek and left a damp patch on his pillow. What a bloody mess this all was. Another tear followed and Bertie found himself sobbing. He was scrawny with hunger and worn out, coping by himself.

He had tried to carry on, working in his shop, but stock was nearly out and nobody had any money. The Huns were everywhere. They watched people like hawks. Bertie, a shy and quiet man, had seen people being beaten up in the lane outside of his house. Beaten so that they screamed for mercy. He had done nothing – could have done nothing

He had seen planes, loaded with bombs, leaving the Airport, powerless to warn England. He and his pals, friends since schoolboys, stood close to each other, afraid and baffled. How could all this have happened to their little island of Guernsey? They had seen tunnels, fortifications and roads ripping up their countryside, destroying their peaceful, rural life.

But, most of all, Bertie was fearful of what Rita would find. He loved her with all his heart. They had just started their married life when Rita and their baby were evacuated to England. Little Rose had been only three years-old. Everything had gone wrong. What if this bloody war went on for another year? Would Rita even want to come back? Suppose she met someone else? Bertie shuddered. No, he couldn't think about that. Things were bad enough. He could not, would not, cope with the idea of Rita not being in his life. Rita returning to him was the only thing that kept him going. The trouble was he had worked so hard before the war. He and Rita had quarrelled. She didn't seem to realise that keeping her in the style she wanted was costing him a fortune, yet he still wanted to look after her. The trouble was, he told Wilf his closest friend, that he happened to love Rita very much. At least she wasn't here now, with no wireless and no one for company with the Germans sucking them dry, day after day.

Today he'd only seen the milkman and old Bretel. If Rita came back he'd make changes. But she would have to give as well as take. Yes, he'd been soft and let people get away with things. He'd have to show her he meant for them to get on. He was keeping the house as nice as he could, beating the carpets, dusting and gardening. He was even doing his own sewing and darning.

The worse thing was the Gestapo, searching houses when and where they liked. It left you feeling your home wasn't yours. But Bertie had carefully saved money for Rita. It would be a surprise for her. He had invented a tea made out of blackberry leaves – with his own recipe. He had sold it at the shop. It had gone down well. Rita would be surprised at how much he had made of himself. But what a mess in town. There had been a bomb exploded, the British had tried to get a U-boat. There was glass everywhere and greenhouse glass replaced the panes.

Rita wouldn't recognise their neighbours, some of them were bags of bones, like skinny children. And, worse, some locals had sold food to the Huns, to get some money. Bertie had certainly found out a thing or two about humanity these last few years.

Old Nico stored carrots, deep in the sand, so that the Germans never found them. Nico made a soup every day. After the war he vowed never to touch another carrot. Some had sold food on the black market. The Huns had stolen cats, dogs and immature vegetable roots. Nothing was safe if it was edible. What a time of it they were all having. Bertie prayed for the end of the war. Then, thank God, in May 1945, it did.

Rita heard the news that morning. The war was over. They were going home. Guernsey was fr ee, at last. But Rita wasn't celebrating. Not by a long way.

Little Rose played outside, running about in the Cotswold fields. They had been lucky. Rita's sister Eileen lived in Gloucestershire and there they had lived since 1940 when they were evacu-ated from Guernsey. They shared the kitchen and Rose slept in Rita's bed. Rose went to the small village school, a house with a flower-filled garden. Rita had a part-time job at the post office, next to the church. They had made a little world of their own. Eileen's husband was in the Army, up in Scotland. Rations were meagre, but they made do well enough.

Still, Rita knew all of this would soon change. Bertie was a good man. He was a hard-working provider. Rita knew that, too. But she had always wanted more. She wanted the life her mother had had – entertaining the Bailiff, holidays in the South of France, shopping trips in London. Bertie wasn't remotely interested in any of those things. Rita had nagged him, scolded him, told him she was fed up. Nothing had made any difference. Bertie liked to save his money, "For our future, Reet," he would say. Surely she could see the sense in that?

Now, Rita was exiled and living in England. And now, there was Lionel. Lionel lived in the Manor House of the village. Lionel always managed to find a few treats for Rita and Rose. Even Eileen had gratefully stored away the fine fruit Lionel gave them from his orchard. Rita never asked Lionel why he wasn't called up, or why he hadn't joined up. She really didn't want to know the reasons. Life was so serious and boring enough, already.

One day Lionel came over, very early in the morning. Eileen was out with little Rose. They had cycled to the village shop to queue for their rations for lunch. Rita's black hair was curled in fashionable finger waves. She had a white skin and sleepy, dark eyes. She was wearing a white, lacy blouse, high-collared at the throat. She went outside to pump some water from the fern-fronded well outside. Lionel, still sitting on his bike, smiled at her over the garden wall.

"Now, then," he said, "there's a sight for sore eyes," and he grinned at her. Rita was first startled, then she blushed. She wished she was wearing the silk stockings some American soldiers, billeted near them, had given to her and Eileen. "Hya, honey!" They had shouted, tossing the wonderful gifts over the hedge. "Wear these and think of us!" Then they had driven off in their Army trucks. They were always doing things like that, the Yanks.

Suddenly, Rita became very aware of Lionel, striding up the path. What was he thinking of? And why did she even begin thinking again of those silk stockings?

"Let me carry that pail," said Lionel, softly. Their hands touched briefly on the pail's handle. Rita swiftly withdrew her hand, leaving Lionel to take all the weight and he carried the water over in to the kitchen. He put the pail down, carefully on the cold flagstone. Outside, the sun shone hotly. In the kitchen, all was cool and shadowed.

"Rita," Lionel blurted, "I want, I have wanted to tell you..." he hesitated, but soon continued, seeing her dark eyes widen and her pale hands shake. "Let me take care of you. Do you really want to leave England and go back to – where is it? Guernsey? Some titchy little island? I'll bet the Germans have run it down. It'll take years and years to live the sort of life I know I can offer you. Right now, Rita. Now, Rita. You and Rose. What do you say?"

132

Rita stumbled, "I, I don't want you to say such things. You have been very kind. I am very grateful. But…" I am married, she wanted to scream. I am married. Lionel really was a fine looking man: tall, slim and sophisticated. He was English and rich. He was everything Bertie wasn't.

Frightened, Rita turned her face away from Lionel. Her profile against the white kitchen wall made his heart leap. What a beauty this one was and she didn't even know it.

Lionel glanced out of the window. Damn it, he could see Eileen and Rose cycling back in the bright sunshine. Already they were nearly at the garden gate.

"Rita," he caught her white hand in his, "just think about what I have said. I meant *every* word. Don't let this chance go. We haven't much time. Let me know your answer, dear. I am waiting. I will always wait." On an impulse he took a chance and kissed the nape of her neck. She didn't flinch.

Lionel ran then, frantically waving goodbye to Eileen as he fled down the gravel path. Rita watched him go. She held on to the opened window casement and waved, her white laced sleeve fluttering as she did so. She didn't take her eyes off the dark haired man until he had cycled out of her sight. Then Lionel was gone.

It was a few weeks later and they had a definite sailing date. Rita had delayed going back to Guernsey. She told Bertie Rose had an illness, then that she needed to help Eileen a little longer. Small, not-quite truths.

Bertie didn't complain. Though his silence and forbearance spoke volumes. He was a Guernseyman, through and through. Yet, Rita knew Bertie loved her. Why, then, did going back to live with him fill her with such dread?

She never did reply to Lionel. Although she thought of him a great deal. Once, she saw him, in the gardens of the Manor House, with his mother. There was an end of war party going on. They were strolling together and laughing. Lavender grew tall and in their gardens were perfect cream roses, tinged with pink.

Rita and Eileen had been invited to the garden party, some time after Lionel's talk of love to her. But neither of them went. Eileen had said, quietly, "Best not, eh, Rita? Best not?"

The crossing over the English Channel was stormy and rough. Little Rose cried out and was sick. Rita comforted her, getting up from her deck chair and making sure her head didn't touch the girl's next to her.

"Move away, darling..." Rita said. Lice, in these circumstances, thrived.

As a seagull cried out, Rita turned and looked over the ship rails. Suddenly, there, five years after she had last set eyes on it, was the pine tree'd headland of Jerbourg. Guernsey shimmered, a lush green and fertile island rising like a mirage out of a turquoise sea. The ship glided silently along the coast. Rita could see the bay of Fermain, Fort George, Havelet and then St Peter Port. Rita wept.

The island of Guernsey looked like paradise. Her own homeland was, at last, in front of her. The white buildings, piled in tiers from harbour to horizon, were bathed in early morning sunshine. It wasn't even seven o'clock yet. But there were throngs of people on the jetty. People were waving, cheering and laughing. The war was well and truly over. Rita ran to collect Rose, holding her and pointing out to her Castle Cornet, Elizabeth College and the tall, church spires. As they looked down amongst the crowds, Rita suddenly spotted Bertie. He was so changed! She had to look twice, but, yes, it was him. He had a careworn, thinner face but still had the stocky figure of a determined man. Yes, that was definitely Bertie.

Grabbing their few belongings, Rita held Rose to her and negotiated the gangplank as best she could. At once, Bertie saw her and fought his way to the front of the crowds. Bertie caught Rita's eye and smiled a wistful smile. He'd lost a few teeth, she thought, and needed a haircut. Five years of hard neglect showed, no doubt about it. Next thing Rita knew, Bertie was at her side. He clung tightly to her and Rose. They said nothing. They both wept. After a minute or two Bertie wiped the tears from her eyes with his roughened hand.

"Thanks for coming home, Reet," he said. His loving face and clear blue, uncomplaining eyes never left hers.

Rita knew, right then, that, yes, she would make a go of it. This would be her thanks to God for getting them all through their darkest doubts, alive and well. Well enough, at least, to have some strength left to even start to think of a future.

"From the shadows, Bertie," smiled Rita, "and into the sunshine?" Then they each took one of Rose's hands and walked along the White Rock harbour. They found a driver with his horse and cart. And, together, they waited patiently to be taken along the Guernsey seafront, to the beginning of their new life.

35 Evacuation

Edwin Bréhaut married Mary on 22 March, 1939. Mary, who was just 19, had travelled to Guernsey from Bury, in Lancashire, at the age of 16 at the insistence of her sisters, Frances and Noreen, and their Guernsey husbands, Jack Goubert and Len Willis. They were concerned that Mary, after living a quiet convent life, would not be suited to work in a Lancashire factory.

So it was that Mary began employment in the Town Hospital (now the home of the Island Police Force) as an auxiliary nurse. Her dark Irish good looks ensured that she was soon snapped up by Edwin (known to his friends as Winno). At the time of her wedding day, Mary was only 19, and Winno was 27. Royal Guernsey Golf Club and L'Ancresse Golf Club members formed a guard of honour with their clubs. Edwin, a three handicap golfer and popular member, had played for Guernsey against Jersey many times.

The young couple made their home at La Blanche Carrière near L'Ancresse. They furnished the rooms with great care from their savings, buying many items in London, where they had their honeymoon.

On 22 February 1940 the young Bréhauts celebrated the birth of their first daughter, Maureen. They settled down, like their many friends and relations, to married life in Guernsey. Edwin worked in the family business of tomato and flower growing, helping his uncle, Alfred Heaume, with packing and carting produce to the UK. It was a good life and they were very happy.

But, in 1940, four months after their baby's birth, Mary and Edwin's lives were turned upside down and were never the same again. For the Second World War had begun in Europe and the little Channel Island of Guernsey was to be occupied by German soldiers.

Evacuation began with only one week's warning, and no information of where they were heading nor where they would end up. Mary, her newborn baby, and Edwin's three sisters, with all their children, gathered a few belongings to board a waiting boat at the White Rock.

The men followed on in the next boat. Edwin, his brother Don, Rex

Green, Roy Sheppard and Gerry Torode all volunteered to join up. Some joined the Army – the Hampshire Regiment – and some the Royal Air Force. Edwin signed on as a member of the Royal Air Force. No sooner had the little family found its feet in the Cotswolds of Gloucestershire, having been joined by a second baby daughter, Yvonne, on 10 May 1942, than Edwin heard he was to be sent overseas.

At this time, 1943, they had no idea of how long their separation would be, no indication of where the overseas post was and faced a dangerously uncertain future.

Edwin and Mary devised a code so that when he wrote to her she would know which 'hot country' he had been sent to. Edwin knew the country was going to be very hot since he had been issued with tropical kit. Once the troops were aboard the warship, talk was that it might be Australia, or Africa. But the young Guernseyman, not yet 30, with a wife and two little children waiting for him in England, woke one day to find himself in the steaming, alien climate of India. And India was not only hot, it was humid, dirty and a long long way from the English Channel. It was to be Edwin's home for three years.

Back in Gloucestershire, Mary shared a house with Edwin's sisters, children, and husbands when on leave. They all stuck together and helped each other. Daily living apart from loved ones was made bearable with companionship of their own country people. And, anyway, there was nothing to be done but to get on with it and pray the war would soon be over.

Once his superiors knew of his Guernsey origins, Edwin was promoted to coxswain of the Air Sea Rescue Unit and he saw many sad, gruesome sights in this demanding, responsible role. The heat, mosquitoes, snakes and strangeness of it all took its toll on Edwin and he suffered a severe attack of malaria, an illness which still returns even today.

All the while, he longed to be at home in Guernsey. He dreamed of the day he could be reunited with Mary and the little girls. Thankfully, the day did at last dawn when the Second World War was declared over. On 9th May 1945 Guernsey was liberated from occupation. Exiled Guernsey people could return (although not until 1946); all was going to be well. But it was not. All was not well for a very long time for Edwin and Mary. Firstly they discovered, like many others, that *every* piece of their furniture and effects had been stolen.

Unable to return to La Blanche Carrière, the family were given temporary accommodation in Edwin's parents' cottage, along with several other relations, while they all searched for new homes or made their old ones habitable. The little girls were confused at being uprooted from the Cotswolds which they had come to think of as home.

All of them had to get to know Winno all over again. Edwin, a Guernseyman through and through, found to his horror that living on a quiet, small island, (very few cars or aeroplanes around in those days!)

Mary, Edwin, Maureen and Yvonne Bréhaut

Edwin and Mary Bréhaut in Australia

137

after the noisy Indian way of life, and RAF routine, was almost impossible. He walked up and down the White Rock, wondering what on earth he was going to do. It was difficult to settle down and on top of that he had to find a civilian job, a home and begin again to save for his family. The long awaited dream had a nightmare edge.

Alfred, Elise and Lilian Heaume, unmarried brothers and sisters, lived at Solidor, the Victorian family home of Adèle Bréhaut, Edwin's mother. Luckily, there was an empty wing, currently occupied by chickens, which could be renovated, and there was a large garden. Edwin could begin work again with Alfred.

So it was agreed, and the family moved in to Solidor. They stayed for more than thirty years. Both Edwin and Mary were pleased that accommodation was available, since their only son, Bruce, was born to them in September 1946.

Everyone who had suffered the same fate as Edwin and Mary found it a struggle to start again and build their lives. The enforced separation caused by the evacuation and service in the Forces made it hard to adjust for this generation of young Guernsey people. The cruel war caused much unseen and misunderstood hardship. This was not always recognised, for those that stayed in the occupied island have more readily received attention to their situation.

Slowly, the harsh, frugal Forties progressed into the easier, more plentiful Fifties. Edwin and Mary completed their family with two more daughters: Margaret in 1950 and Elizabeth in 1953.

Their beloved son, Bruce, contracted meningitis at 15 months old. Although Bruce was left profoundly deaf, Edwin and Mary thanked God he had been spared to them. Bruce went on to live a richly fulfilled life, leaving all who knew him the better for having met him.

Edwin, now 82 and Mary, 75 recently visited Melbourne, Australia, staying with Frances Goubert until she died, aged 80. The Bréhauts have many grandchildren and great-grandchildren and keep well, living quietly in the Vale. Their story is but one of many, but should still be told.

For there is Another Long Goodbye, and it is of the sorrow and disruption caused to families for many years after a war has ended. That Edwin and Mary survived together, and their children and grandchildren have inherited the right to live in Guernsey, is a fine achievement.

But let us remember the years spent away and the sacrifices made for all of us by Guernsey people.

36 Ma Normandie

July 2004

Guernsey people have a strong sense of identity. We recognise our islanders wherever we go. "There", we say, "is a Guern, if ever I saw one." Determined, stubborn, strong as an ox. And that's just the women!

I lived in Ouistreham, Normandy, for six months. Every day I saw men and women who reminded me of my father, my family and my great grandparents. The long seawall in front of our rented house made me think of Pembroke and L'Ancresse. As I watched the sea come in, wave after salty-blue wave, I yearned for Guernsey.

Yet, if you are going to be exiled, Normandy, France, is probably the best place to be. For the life there is just as I recall in my childhood. People live with the seasons, with the weather, and are quietly resourceful, just like us. Fishing is still a living; small gardens are filled with flowers and vegetables; chickens scratch about.

We were in France whilst my daughter and son-in-law studied at Caen University. They are lawyers and I looked after their two small daughters. They learned about ancient Guernsey history: the Queen, the Crowned Monarch of the English throne, being 'Duke of Normandy' is what gives us our own freedom, our protection and our own unique identity.

800 years ago, King John, whose Norman French ancestors had conquered England, promised Guernsey independence and the right to continue governing ourselves. Guernsey confirmed her allegiance to the English Crown. To this day, Guernsey remains a possession of the English crown, though we have never been invaded by the English.

Our laws are the old laws of the Norman French. They are written in the earliest known books as *Tres ancien Coutumier* (very old, customary). Our agents of the Crown are called 'Bailiffs'. There were bailiffs all over Normandy at one time.

When Elizabeth I, Queen of England (1558-1603) came to the throne, she was interested in knowing more about her islands. A book by William Terrien, 1578, *Commentaire du droit Civil observe au pays et duche de Normandie* (Commentary on the civil law observed in the country and duchy of Normandy), was approved as representative of the laws and it remains the root of all Guernsey's laws today. Elizabeth also granted the island exemption from English tax and independence judicially and administratively.

Guernsey was originally part of the Duchy of Normandy. In 1204, 800 years ago this year, the Duchy was lost to France and became a possession of the English Crown. But Guernsey, now an Anglo-Norman island, is proud and independent, with our own laws, traditions and offices of state. Whilst I was there I also learned about more recent history and Guernsey's links with France.

For instance, after the Cambrai battle, France 1917, and heavy losses of young, largely inexperienced Guernseymen, General De Lisle wrote to the Bailiff:

I want to convey to the Guernsey Authorities my very high appreciation of the valuable services rendered by the Royal Guernsey Light Infantry. They carried out all they were asked to do with a completeness that pleased me very much.

He went on to report:

The Germans in their heavy surprise attack, pierced our line to the south…the enemy entered the village of Les rues Vertes. It was the Royal Guernsey Light Infrantry which recovered this village twice…against seven German attacks, with the Germans superior strength and very superior artillery.

On the night of 1st December, with enemy on three sides, it was the Royal Guernsey Light Infantry which covered our withdrawal.

Guernsey has every reason to feel the greatest pride in her sons and I am proud to have them under me, fighting alongside my staunch veterans of three years' fighting experience." He closed by saying, "I regret the casualties were heavy, a further proof, if any were needed, that they fought magnificently.

Cambrai was the end of a generation in Guernsey and the island was stunned by the length of the casualty lists. There was not a parish which had not lost its sons.

And, whilst we were there, France celebrated, as they do every year, the D-Day Normandy landings in the Second World War, and their liberation from Nazi Germany.

Sometimes, as I took the children to the beach to look at the rockpools and paddle our feet, there would be a gathering by a monument at the top of a beach. Once, we went to investigate, at Courselles-sur-mer. A highly decorated Scottish man, in his seventies, was making an emotional speech. The Courselle mayor was there, and hundreds of people, Scottish, French and many nationalities, bowed their heads as prayers were said. As the regimental flags were lowered 'The Marseillaise' and 'God Save the Queen' were played by a small band on the windy pier.

Coronation, 1911

I found myself in tears as I turned to look at the beach and imagined thousands of young men – 18, 19 years-old, some of them – storming up the sands to be instantly killed. Their comrades had had to race on ahead, but now, here they were: old men come back to say, "You will never be forgotten."

On Sunday, 4th June, 2000 my son-in-law, Gordon Dawes, and I, with my eldest granddaughter went to see the opening of the new Pegasus Bridge Museum. Prince Charles, Prince of Wales, was coming to open it.

The day was very hot. Crowds, French and English, stood ten deep. Prince Charles made a good speech, telling of the importance of Pegasus Bridge, which began the liberation of France. Airborne troops (the 'Red Berets') had glided in over the Caen canal to capture the bridge so enabling the allies to begin the Normandy landings and advance. So many lives were lost, but this was the beginning of victory and freedom for France.

Prince Charles had just come from Dunkirk and the last reunion of the little ships. He stopped and spoke to every single Red Beret veteran, as they waited in the searing sun, taking his time, obviously knowledgeable. Then he left, waving to us all. I felt very proud that he would be Guernsey's next Duke of Normandy.

Whether you like the current Royal family or count yourself as a monarchist or not, is neither here nor there. Whilst we are an English Crown possession, we do not need party politics, nor a Member of Parliament sitting in Westminster to speak for us. We speak for ourselves, we govern ourselves. We keep our identity, which is precious beyond all earthly gain.

To lose our laws and customs, and our golden link to the Crown would, and of this be quite sure, render us vulnerable and adrift in increasingly hostile seas.

But I am not concerned. Guernsey people are not known for their docility, to be led like tamed mules. No, we are islanders, stubborn donkeys, with a remarkable history of self worth and strength. Neither will we, ever, lightly hand over our extraordinary island to the British Government. Let the present States of Guernsey note, if it ever decides to embrace party politics, with deference to a British prime minister: Just try us.

37 Plum Puddings

December 2003

It is just before Christmas, in the Fifties, and preparations are well under way. My grandmother has made suety plum puddings, one each for all her family. Tomato chutney, Guernsey pickles and purple sloe gin slowly marinade in the larder. Jams and jars full of summer's fruit wait deliciously on the paper-lined shelves.

We sort out our box of trimmings, ready for the big day. Our father will go to the market to get our tree, smelling of pine. We have discovered where our presents are hidden, but we don't let on. They are in the attic of our great-uncle's Victorian house. Although it is wrapped in brown paper the scent of a 'Saville' gift set, complete with powdery bath cubes, vies with the smell of cooking apples, stored in boxes for the winter. I hope I have got the doll I want that I have seen in the window of Mrs Self's toyshop on the Bridge.

The coal fires blaze as cold Winter bites in. All the rooms without fireplaces are freezing, save for the kitchen where the warm Aga radiates. There is a light dusting of snow outside. The greenhouses are cold and empty now, the soil has been cleaned ready for the new seedlings, early in the new year.

We go for long walks along L'Ancresse common and the deserted beaches, starting from Les Amarreurs, Ladies bay, Chouet, Pembroke and L'Ancresse itself. The island is ours again after the summer visitors have gone. Rock climbing in the chill wind makes our cheeks rosy. Gulls sweep the grey sky and we wonder how they survive. They dip into the icy sea for their dinner. As the rain begins to pelt down we run to keep warm, pulling our coats closer to us. We never take umbrellas or wear Wellington boots. Anyway, we call those "seaboots" and you wear those for wading to and from fishing boats. You can't rockclimb in seaboots. When we get home, we huddle in front of the fire and roast windfall chestnuts. The wireless plays 'Children's Hour' and we thaw out to David Davis telling us a story.

At school we have made our paper chains, with sticky paste and coloured strips, and sung our Carols. The deputy head boy of the Vale

143

School has a beautiful voice. He sings 'In the Deep Midwinter' so wonderfully that I never like another rendering quite so much again.

"Remember," says our teacher, "when you wake up on Christmas morning, before you've opened your presents, to say 'Happy Birthday' to Jesus. Because that's what Christmas Day is for." The little crib we have made is in pride of place in the front of the classroom. It is made of papier mache and carefully hand-painted.

The trimmings are up, the tree decorated with candles and silvery ribbons of Lametta foil. We've put spiky green holly, gathered in the lanes, all around great-grandfather Heaume's picture. My mother says he can join in because she always sees him smile when we do that. By the fireside is a basket full of pine cones we've collected on our walks. On the other side logs are piled up high.

Mr Bohan, my father's friend, has given us his annual present of enormous white and cream pom-pom chrysanthemums. They are called 'American Beauty', grown for the Covent Garden Christmas market. Ever more their pungent citrus scent reminds me of Christmas.

Gradually, our store of food grows. And by the time the December feast draws near, mincemeat for the pies is made. My mother buys unheard of luxuries – a bumper box of biscuits, and boxes of chocolates with *two* layers! There is a tin of Quality Street and boxes of dates, which nobody eats. Bowls of nuts appear on a little table, set up with whisky and brandy and glasses turned upside down on a tray, for people dropping in.

We live near enough to the Vale Church to hear its bells and the Carol singers come round in the evenings. My parents always give them some money. We ask them to sing 'Good King Wenceslas', and 'Silent Night', my favourite.

Great-uncle Alfred and great-aunt Elise never make much of Christmas. Great-aunt Elise will kill and pluck one of her plumpest chickens, sitting on a chair outside to do so. They'll eat this with his cabbage, cauliflower and winter-stored carrots. As a treat she buys Kelliers chocolate fudge fingers and he will light the fire in the dining-room in the morning instead of waiting until four o'clock – just for Christmas Day.

And so, at last, Christmas Eve arrives. Shops are open late for the many people working. It is not a public holiday. Christmas Day and Boxing Day are the only days off work. We see people on the bus with a tree under one arm and bags of parsley and thyme, their unplucked bird poking out of the shopping bag. In the Town market turkeys hang in feathery rows and there are whole hams and game, sausages and patés.

Tony Ozanne, Christmas, 1947

Midnight Mass is magical. I love the candlelight, the singing and the message of hope. Just for once we all forget our troubles as the celebration begins.

In our home we dress in our best clothes, sometimes in jumpers and cardigans knitted especially for Christmas Day. The presents were opened first thing. I do have the doll and we have books, comic annuals (my brother's is *Rupert*), handkerchiefs pinned to their boxes, chocolates and, of course, scented bath cubes.

In the Aga the stuffed chicken roasts, potatoes all around it. The table is set with a white cloth, patterned with red cherries (the "Christmas Day tablecloth"). The fires are lit, the best china brought out.

Relatives arrive and the grown-ups have sherry. All their faces go pink. The men have been doing the Christmas morning round to each other's houses. They laugh loudly and say silly things, winking. We play with our new toys without quarrelling. The grandfather clock ticks, the fires crackle and the cold wind blows outside without anyone noticing.

At last we sit down and pull our crackers. We put on our paper hats and read the riddles. After soup, made with preserved tomato and shallots, the bird is ceremoniously carved. Great Uncle Alfred's vegetables steam in their serving dishes. Beer and red wine, only ever bought at Christmas, is poured. We have Guppy's orange squash.

Our grandmother's plum pudding is duly served with Guersey cream and custard. There is fruit: apples from our trees, tangerines and tinned peaches (quite a luxury). We don't finish our meal until the middle of the afternoon.

In the evening we play cards and memory games in front of the fire. There is no television but we listen to music on the wireless. Nearly all the adults go to sleep.

Just after Christmas, in 1947, my mother read us a story by the warm fireside. It was very quiet and the baby was asleep. Just then a shattering crash made us rush to the conservatory. Through a gaping hole in its glass roof we could see a black sky and flurries of snow, so deep it had brought down the panes.

My parents opened the back door to find a snowfall of some two feet. We thought this was excellent! And next morning we wanted to make a snowman. Bur first of all my father had to clear a path with his spade. The snow came up to his knees!

So, in the deep mid-winter, we look forward once more to our Christmas feast. This year, perhaps more than ever, we all deserve at least one day of Peace on Earth and to wish goodwill to all mankind.

38 Bruce

July 2005

Bruce arrived in September 1946. A fortune teller in India had told my father that his next child would be a boy and that he would be special. Indeed, he was.

A blond and bonny baby, all was well until the time when Bruce suffered meningitis at eighteen months old. Tests soon proved to my anguished and anxious parents that Bruce had been left profoundly deaf. They took him to Harley Street specialists in London but at that time there was no further treatment available and no operation would help. Hearing aids could not assist him and so Bruce faced life without one of the six crucial senses we all take for granted.

Before long the problem of schooling for Bruce arose. He was doted on by my great-aunt Elise who had no children of her own. She was very much against his going away to England. However, that was the only option open then for Bruce and the family.

Today, deaf and hard of hearing children will be able to attend the new school for children with special needs in the Forest. Now, I wonder how different life would have been if Bruce could have stayed in Guernsey.

However, there were two other boys attending The Royal School for the Deaf in Margate, Kent and it was decided that that was where Bruce would be sent. But the wrench for us all three times a year for three terms for the next ten years was heartbreaking. Aged only six, my brother was in effect attending a boarding school away and it was initially very difficult to explain to him why he had to leave us, his four sisters, mother and father. It was very hard on everyone.

When he was around eight years-old Bruce asked me what hearing was like. And, why was he the only one in the family who couldn't hear? I tried to explain sounds. For a time he was very angry and felt isolated.

Gradually, though, Bruce accepted his life and made the best of it. The school gave him a wonderful education and great confidence. The boys and girls were encouraged to lip-read and join in the hearing world rather than only use sign language. This stood Bruce in good stead and we always spoke to Bruce normally, using our voices but with lots of animated descriptions with our hands.

However, Bruce and his deaf friends had a rapid sign language of their own, some of it coded and a kind of shorthand. You had to be very quick to keep up with Bruce in full flow and a room with him and his school friends would be the noisiest imaginable. Dumb didn't come into it.

He had a wonderful sense of humour and mischief, sometimes using his deafness to tease someone. There was a man he didn't care for who always made huge signs and spoke silently in exaggerated and slow fashion. Bruce detested being spoken to as if he was an idiot. So, one day in a workshop where the radio played loudly all day – but Bruce knew when it was switched off because he had a phenomenally aware sense of vibration – he waited for silence then clapped loudly and shouted the man's name, causing him to drop his dish of paint which crashed to the floor, spilling all the liquid. When the man angrily rounded on Bruce he put on an innocent look and said, "But I didn't *know* the noise had stopped. I am deaf!"

All of his sisters played their different parts in looking out for Bruce. When we were little I used to go the pictures with him. He loved a good cowboy film, Laurel and Hardy and the Marx brothers. All very animated films. In the dark of the cinema, Bruce would prod my ribs with his elbow wanting to know what was going on. So I had to follow the plot and tell Bruce the story simultaneously. This has left me with a lifelong ability to analyse and communicate at the same time and possibly also accounts for my nosiness and good memory.

He left school at sixteen and Bruce worked at Tektronix for a while and made good friends. People were very kind and he had an engaging manner and was very handsome. But soon he began to long for the open air and to work out of doors. So he joined R G Falla and worked on the new harbour and the Princess Elizabeth Hospital. He became very skilled and was proud of his contribution to Guernsey's architecture.

Many of his workmates learnt some of the sign language for the deaf and Bruce made deep friendships. He liked his pint and on one occasion whilst at the Royal CI Yacht Club enjoying his leisure, Oliver Reed walked in. Oliver began to challenge the men to an arm wrestling match. He was not a small man – in fact, he was something of a gentle giant. Soon Bruce joined in the fun and offered 'the best of three' matches with

Oliver. Bruce won! From then on whenever he wanted to, he proudly produced a signed note from Oliver Reed saying, "This b****** is stronger than me!" Both larger than life, they ended the evening the best of friends.

Because of the heightened sense of vibration, Bruce had a rare gift – much as the deaf classical musician Evelyn Glennie has, of being able to feel rhythm. Once, at a dance, Bruce conducted the live band because he could feel the music through the wooden floorboards. He always knew when there was something wrong with his car and where it was. He could feel the abnormality through the steering wheel. He would go to a garage and astonish the mechanics by lifting the bonnet and pointing to the exact problem.

And when we were young we would lie in the grass and he told me a plane was coming. I looked up to a vacant blue sky. "No," I would reply, puzzled. But, sure enough, slowly and just a speck at first, a plane would fly over. How did he know? "I felt it through the ground," he told me.

Because the fluid normally present in the canals of the ears had effectively been burnt out by meningitis, Bruce was never seasick. Once, on a ferry to France, the sea was so rough that even the crew were sick. Bruce helped himself at the bar, smiled at everyone and, when the boat docked, disembarked fresh as a daisy, to enjoy his stay in France. He could also endure great heights without fear. He used this capacity to earn extra 'danger money' and loved the view of the island from the highest crane on the White Rock.

Bruce had no social barriers. He would walk up to quarrelling people and tell them to make up. Once, sitting in a parked car and squabbling, a couple told me that Bruce had banged on their window and told them to stop being unhappy and made a smiley face at them. They were so taken aback they had to laugh and Bruce laughed with them.

His laughter and sense of fun were wonderfully infectious. In a room full of people Bruce would use his eyes and tell me which person he thought was obnoxious, who was flirting, who he thought was ugly and who he fancied. It was very difficult to keep a straight face when he was around and absolutely impossible to ignore him.

The only thing that exasperated Bruce was people treating him as deaf and dumb. He would get furious with that person. "I can understand *you* but you can't understand *me* although you can hear! Who's dumb?" he quite rightly said. And it is a shame that the high technology we have

149

Mary and Edwin Bréhaut with Bruce, aged 4, outside the Harley Street specialist's clinic where his deafness was confirmed

Bruce, aged 17, loved to party and was very popular – and handsome

Lady Hailsham presents 10 year-old Bruce with a prize for progress at the Royal School for the Deaf, Margate

At just 18 months old, Bruce was diagnosed as profoundly deaf after suffering meningitis

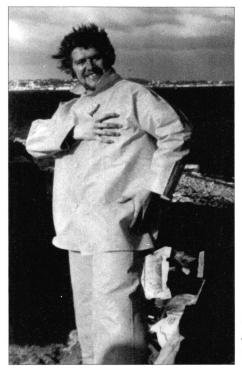

Bruce, aged 40, working on Jethou. He went to and fro daily by helicopter

151

now: e-mails, telephone texting, the internet, sophisticated cameras etc weren't around when he was growing up and had become an adult. These things are all so helpful to the deaf when it comes to communicating.

There is an operation available now which was being done in America when Bruce was in his thirties which helps his specific condition. But Bruce refused it. He was worried how he might react to sound after all those years. He had adapted to his world and the deaf society in Guernsey and decided to stay as he was.

On the occasions when I didn't understand him Bruce was disappointed and impatient with me. He would take out a pen and paper and write out what he wanted to say, giving me a withering look as if to say "You are stupid!" Sometimes he would write the words slowly and carefully, letting me know that that is how he felt – being told something in slow motion as though his very good brain wasn't somehow working.

He had a huge interest in general knowledge, people and ideas. We could literally talk for hours and would paint and draw endlessly. When we very young we would take turns to make up a story – usually something thrilling along the lines of King Solomon's mines and adventure stories that ended with 'cliff hangers' for the next day.

When I heard that Bruce had had an accident at the Princess Elizabeth Hospital new building I wasn't too worried. Bruce hadn't heard the warning beep as an excavator backed toward him and he was trapped by the leg. It had been unpleasant and a shock, but we didn't expect his recovery to take too long.

So, a few months later when Bruce began to lose weight and was obviously not well we did begin to worry. The leg wouldn't mend. There was some circulatory trouble – Bruce, very unusually, lacked energy.

Just before Christmas, 1990, Bruce saw his doctor who thought that he was over a flu bout and able to go to Margate for a reunion with his school friends from The Royal School for the Deaf. In the meantime our grandmother, aged 100 years, died and Bruce attended her funeral, as we all did. He didn't seem at all well and told us that he had pains in his back. But he still wanted to go to the reunion.

On January 4th 1991 my parents took Bruce to the airport and he waved, telling them not to worry. He would be back soon. He attended the reunion, and in fact had a very good party, glad to see all of his old school friends.

The next morning Bruce had breakfast but wanted a walk, telling his friend's wife he wouldn't be long. But soon Bruce needed help. He went into a garage and asked the petrol assistant if he could phone for a doctor. The assistant offered him a chair but when he returned Bruce had died. He was 44.

At Bruce's funeral at the Vale Church, the late Reverend Peter Simpson shed tears as he spoke of "and in heaven the deaf shall hear." Hundreds of people in the congregation wept with him. Then Rev Simpson told us of Bruce's strong character, telling us that *we* were the one's with a problem; he could, after all, understand *us*. So there was laughter and that was Bruce: tears and laughter in equal measure. And a life lived with great courage, warmth and humour. He was very special and can never be replaced.

39 First Home

We are helping our son, whilst he fits out a new flat. It is in the old quarter of Town, in an old house, so there are decent sized rooms and it is light and airy, and in the centre of the busy Town life.

In 1963 we had to save up for a deposit and for everything in our first little home. That, or you could get things on Hire Purchase, much frowned upon by Guernsey people in those days. Although, I did get some things from a 'Club Book', which my father counted as the same thing as HP, anyway.

Our first home cost £2,000. It was semi-detached with a small back garden and we loved it. Mrs Wakeford's store was just over the way and we overlooked a meadow. L'Islet and Les Amarreurs were a few minutes walk from Sandy Hook.

The only thing fitted in our kitchen was the sink. So, we bought a kitchen cabinet. It had shelves with glass paned doors, and a flap that hung down for use as a working surface. At the bottom was a cupboard for saucepans and crockery. We thought we were very up-to-date and had our first meal in the kitchen, a chair either side of the kitchen cabinet flap, whilst we were in the midst of decorating.

Next we bought an electric oven and sometime later a fridge (with no freezer). Few people had fridges then, or washing machines, tumble driers, dishwashers or microwaves – all of which have been fitted as standard in our son's flat.

We had a coal fire in the sitting room and no radiators or central heating anywhere else. Washing and ironing used to take days, depending on the weather. Handwash was done every morning in the sink when the babies were small. Nappies were sterilised in pails and rinsed out and hung to dry on the washing line. Only the well-off used disposable nappies. My son was born in November and one December day I took his nappies off the line frozen stiff. They were like large white playing cards. I carried them indoors in a freezing pile to air on a clothes horse before the crackling fire.

I bought a complete set of stainless steel cutlery from Leale's, on the

154

Bridge, one knife, fork and spoon a week. Luckily they didn't discontinue the range because it took months to get the whole set, including fish knifes. We used to go to Brennan and the Co-op, which is now 'Travelmaker' at the top of the market steps in Town. We bought our kitchen table, it was covered in Formica and so I used to put a white linen cloth over it for dinner parties.

Tony and Michael service the Mini

For my first dinner party in our little house I used the china dinner ('Tumbling Leaves') and coffee services we had been given as wedding presents. I produced *paté de foie* canapés which we ate in the sitting room with aperitifs, because I didn't have enough china then to have 'starters'. Then *boeuf bourguignon* (cooked in a Copco cast-iron casserole dish that I won in a national competition [2nd prize]) and which I still have and use to this day. Then lemon meringue pie (my mother-in-law's recipe) with home-made shortcrust pastry and Guernsey cream. We finished with coffee (real coffee made in our Russell Hobbs percolater, another wedding present). We watched the bubbles through its glass lid

155

as it produced a delicious aroma and this was our entertainment before we could afford a television.

Piece by piece we gradually added things to our home: a secondhand three piece suite and a solid mahogany Ercol coffee table with spindly legs (dead modern in those days). From a small scullery that used to be a tiny kitchen, my husband fitted a new bathroom, plumbing and all, which replaced the outside loo.

I cleaned the kitchen floor with a mop and a product called 'Dual' to get a nice shine on our linoleum floor. But my builder cousin was horrified saying Dual would collect grime and take ages to remove. In fact, I don't see Dual advertised anymore. And, anyway, today's generation seem to go for ceramic tiles and wood or wood-effect floors. My builder cousin was also enraged with women wearing stiletto heels (all the rage then) as they pierced almost any flooring with little holes and ruined it.

Ovens were stripped and cleaned every Sunday. Housework was expected to be done in the mornings, ready for any visitors in the afternoon. Washing on the line after Monday indicated a lazy housewife and Tuesday morning was for ironing.

Our son is fitting smart blinds on his windows. We had white nets and fitted, lined, curtains. Good curtains were a major expense, even with no swags or fancy pelmets. They were as important as the colour of your wallpaper (always wallpaper, then) and your carpets.

Fitted carpets were the height of fashion and cost a fortune. We just had a beige linoleum and a large green carpet square with beige pattern in the first sitting room. But we hired a black and white television, had a black telephone hanging on the wall and had added a teak bookcase I got in a Brennan sale.

I mostly bought in sales. Penguin publishers were doing a really good range of paperbacks then, which I devoured and hoarded like treasure. As a young teenager, my husband had bought a Phillips portable record player that looked like a suitcase. It opened up and revealed a mono-speaker. It had a pick-up arm, that swung over the record to begin it and an automatic record stacker. We'd play Count Basie, the Modern Jazz Quartet, Peggy Lee and, later, the Beatles who were just getting known.

We had no car, but a motorbike. Our first car was a second hand Ford Esquire. I helped to earn the down-payment bunching iris in the kitchen for my father. The mortgage was almost crippling and we didn't have a holiday or a new car for many years. Later, we bought a Mini from some money my husband won from the Lottery in a syndicate at Tektronix.

But there was always work in the greenhouses and packing sheds. Tektronix changed many lives but Horticulture and Tourism flourished then and dominated career choice.

Now, wandering around B& Q and Homemaker, we marvel at how you can buy whole bathrooms in one go! And the colour and range of kitchen units is awe-inspiring, if baffling. Young people have no qualms about ripping out unfashionable furnishings, even though they are perfectly functionable.

Yet, would we change our simpler beginnings for the pace, stress and pressure of today's young homemakers? And, they are living and bringing their children into a Guernsey so rapidly changing. Thankfully, they have traditions that still count and family links are still very strong.

Guernsey's island life is much more than annual shows and the organised events like Viaer Marche, although it is good that these are continued. It is about shared values and strong, independent characters.

These things ensure that the spirit of Guernsey is still very much alive and kicking.

40 An Awfully Big Event

July 2006

It was something we had been awaiting for years. Now, at long last, it was about to happen. We could scarcely believe it. The momentous time drew nearer and our excitement reached such a pitch we could barely eat or sleep properly. It was June, 1966 and the unimaginable event might just become true.

No, not just that England was about to win the World Cup, but that our longed for baby was about to be born. She was due and was born right on the expected date: July 7th. We brought her home on a nice sunny day and began the business of tending to a brand new first baby.

In the meantime, England won game after game and headed, almost unthinkably, toward the World Cup Final game against Germany on July 30th. So there I was, with a baby daughter, a few days old, and not having a clue as to what to do whilst Tony sat on the edge of his seat each time a game was shown on television, lost to the world.

Meantime, I sat on the edge of my chair, peering into the newborn's cot, trying to make out whether our new baby was hungry, tired, wet or windy. Each time I asked Tony what he thought he looked at me blankly. After all, as our little girl neared three weeks old, he had to take in the fact that Jimmy Greaves had been left out of the England team by Alf Ramsey.

The big names of today like Beckham, Rooney and Owen, were then, of course, Bobby Moore, Geoff Hurst, Martin Peters, Roger Hunt, Gordon Banks, the Charlton brothers and Nobby Stiles. And, of course, Tony watched all the games he could.

I knew little about football, but enough to know that it had been a long time and perhaps would be a long time in the future until England got so close to winning the World Cup. So, as I changed nappies (terry towelling – cleansed by soaking in a bucket of Napisan, then boiled in a Burco boiler, rinsed and hung out each morning on the line – rain or shine) and immersed feeding bottles in Milton steriliser; hand washed baby clothes, plus our own clothes, I did try to be patient.

Mind you, Tony was ace at getting the baby to sleep. Somehow, as

Alison Ozanne, three weeks old, 1966

Bobby Moore with the World Cup

soon as he held her, she got a really calm look and immediately nodded off. On the very day, though, that the final game was to be played, the baby decided to have a colic attack. Nervously, I bathed her in a white plastic baby bath on the kitchen table. She cried throughout.

Tony was practically paralysed by now, staring at our black and white telly, a small box sitting in the corner. It was a Saturday afternoon and he was watching Grandstand, introduced by David Coleman. I realised that it would be no good asking him anything. I placed the baby in her cot, but it was no good. I took her out again and gave her two teaspoons of Dinnefords anti-colic stuff. She gulped down some, spat out the rest and continued to cry.

It seemed she would never stop. Anxiously, I went into the kitchen with her. Tony firmly closed the door of the lounge. I began to cry to myself, feeling quite alone and utterly unable to help my child. She looked so tiny and vulnerable. I felt very aware of her complete dependency on me. Then it came to me: I should take the baby for a walk.

So, I wrapped her up, put her into her pram, put on a cardigan and walked down the lane, toward the path alongside the L'Islet pine trees. Then I turned around and went far as Ashby-de-la-Zouch tearooms, just before Les Amarreurs. Happily, the walk worked. The baby stopped crying. She burped loudly several times and fell asleep, her little red face at last looked a peaceful pink.

Swiftly, I headed back to Sandy Hook and our semi-detached house. There was hardly any traffic since anyone who had a television was inside, riveted to the screen.

So why was Tony running around our small garden shouting "Yes! Yes!" and then punching the air? You guessed: because the game was over and, unbelievably, incredibly, England had won the World Cup Final – 4-2.

Next day all the newspapers were full of the pictures of captain Bobby Moore, brandishing the cup, sitting on his team-mates' shoulders. Like David Beckham, Bobby Moore was a charismatic icon of talent and good looks.

Yes, the day England won the World Cup, 1966, remains a Technicolor memory of Bobby Moore's fair hair and the team's red and white shirt and shorts. Who can forget Nobby Stiles running around the stadium, ecstatically, without his front teeth, kissing all and sundry? I wonder what those World Cup heroes would be earning now?

Quite unbelievably, that was all forty years ago. Those were the days when Fort George had just happened and the 'skyscraper' block at Cour du Parc had been built for the grand sum of £120,000.

Not only did we not have colour television, we didn't have mobile phones or e-mails. Newspapers, radio and now television were our main suppliers of news and events.

And, yes, July 1966 was an exciting time and one which we will never forget. My baby turned out just fine (I had got the hang of things by the time her brother arrived in 1967). Of course, our dear Guernsey has irrevocably changed over the years, but here's hoping for England in the coming weeks. What a difference: LCD, HD screens, Plasma television etc., etc. It is going to be like you are actually there this time.

So much for 1966 and all the many changes we have witnessed down all the years. And, for me, Kenneth Wolstenholme uttered the most significant of all words: "Some people are on the pitch. They think it's all over...It is now."